The Presidency on Trial

Stuart Gerry Brown, professor of American studies at the University of Hawaii, brings to this study many years of association with political campaigns and involvement with party policy making. He was a campaign associate of Adlai Stevenson in every election year from 1952 to 1960; he was a member of the Civil Rights Panel of the Democratic Advisory Council from 1957 to 1960; and he was a campaign consultant to Robert Kennedy's staff in 1968.

THE PRESIDENCY
ON TRIAL

Robert Kennedy's 1968 Campaign and Afterwards

Stuart Gerry Brown

HONOLULU
THE UNIVERSITY PRESS OF HAWAII
1972

Library of Congress Catalog Card Number 70-175162
ISBN 0-8248-0202-0
Copyright © 1972 by Stuart Gerry Brown
Manufactured in the United States of America

Contents

becomes passionate commitment. RFK builds a new coalition of the concerned, the poor, the black, and the young. RFK's empathy with blacks, chicanos, and Indians. Momentum lost after 1968.

PART II
Afterwards

Preface

As the days and years go by, Robert Kennedy's assassination takes on greater, not less significance in the current history of American political leadership. His brief, tragic campaign for the Presidency in 1968, with its radical thrust at the crucial issues of war, poverty, race, and youth, appears more, not less relevant to the condition of the United States. His promise of leadership and his spirit of reconciliation are more, not less necessary for the survival of the democratic presidential system. This book recalls that campaign not in biographical but in political and ethical terms, and tries to "point the moral" that "adorns the tale." The perspective is not the past but the future, especially the immediate future which will determine whether the Presidency can and will prove itself in its time of greatest tribulation since the Civil War.

In two earlier books (*Conscience in Politics: Adlai E. Stevenson in the 1950's*, 1961, and *The American Presidency: Leadership, Partisanship, and Popularity*, 1966) I have advanced the thesis that the presidential system works best when the President and his leading opponents (the "executive" of each party) in election campaigns— and afterwards—propose, explain, develop, and exert political leadership for policies and programs intended to deal directly with problems, and ills, of American society, not hesitating to take divisive positions. I have discussed, with detailed historic examples, the often irresistible—or at least unresisted—temptation by such "executives" to avoid doing just that by sometimes very skillful uses of politics. This book raises sharply the question whether there is any

viii

longer a "living option" to practice presidential politics at the expense of presidential leadership. I think not.

I am indebted to Harlan Cleveland, Reuel Denney, Guy Kirkendall, Floyd Matson, Dorothy Arnof, and Dorothy Sickels for reading all or parts of the manuscript and giving me valuable advice. I am grateful, too, to Frank Mankiewicz, Arthur Schlesinger, Jr., Eric Sears, and Lee Stetson for various kinds of assistance and encouragement.

Parts of Chapters 2, 5, and 6 were read as lectures to the students and faculty of several Australian universities. And I should like to express warm gratitude for courtesy and colleagueship to B. F. Dalton of James Cook University, North Queensland; Manning Clark, B. F. Crisp, and Hector Kinloch of the Australian National University; and L. C. F. Turner and Roger Thompson of the Royal Military College; as well as Frank Willcock of the Australian-American Foundation.

S. G. B.

Honolulu
12 September 1971

PART I

Robert Kennedy's 1968 Campaign

*To find the true balance between security and freedom,
between initiative and anarchy, between tolerance and
conformity, to organize vast patience and understanding for
the peaceful resolution of conflicts, to communicate the
material and spiritual goals of life by the example of a
superior system of self-management and self-discipline,
these are the tasks of democratic statesmanship in our tense
times. And these are tasks for adults, not children, for
reason, not emotion, for faith, not fear.*

—ADLAI E. STEVENSON

*But past error is no excuse for its own perpetuation.
Tragedy is a tool for the living to gain wisdom, not a guide
by which to live. Now as ever, we do ourselves best justice
when we measure ourselves against ancient tests, as in the
Antigone of Sophocles: "All men make mistakes, but a
good man yields when he knows his course is wrong, and
repairs the evil. The only sin is pride."*

—ROBERT F. KENNEDY

ONE

Introduction

These are the times that try the souls of Presidents. Tom Paine would recognize the language. Perhaps, taking a look at his country after some two hundred years, he would even be willing to lend us his words. In less troubled times than ours, that original American radical was a scornful critic of the character and policies of the first President.

But more important than the present-day testing of the mettle of Presidents is the testing of the presidential system itself. Only a few years ago that system was not in question and did not appear likely ever to be seriously taxed. But its very successes seem to have put it in jeopardy. It is now not only fair but necessary to ask whether the presidential system can blunt the attacks of its more virulent enemies, satisfy the legitimate claims of the blacks, of other minorities like the Puerto Ricans, the Mexican Americans, and the Indians, and of the white poor, yet reassure the great middle-class majority by bringing crime and violence under control —all this while working to diminish the nation's and the world's fear of ultimate disaster from environmental pollution and war.

The alternative to the survival of the "system" is neither the anarchy so devoutly hoped for by some of the younger —and a few of the older—radicals nor a golden day of "participatory democracy." The "greening of America" is only another version of the Rousseauistic illusion of natural benevolence. The real alternative to the presidential system is a mean and narrow repressive state, acting in the name of American ideals to bring an end to the free politics which lets them flourish. It is not helpful to talk of a "coming American fascism" or to borrow slogans and catchwords

3

from the experiences of other countries at other times. The blunt fact of the American situation is that far too many Americans like what they have too well to be vulnerable to the New Left revolutionaries. If polarization is allowed to run the logic of its course it will not be the radical minority that will overcome. ("We shall *not* overcome," Jack Newfield has already concluded.)[1] It will be the big majority, as Tocqueville foretold more than a century and a quarter ago, that will finally impose its tyranny.

There is no certainty that any President could "turn this country around," as Robert Kennedy proposed to do in 1968. What is certain is that the course toward some form of democratically sanctioned repression will not be altered without effective presidential leadership. The President must adopt radical programs to bring an end to ghetto and rural poverty, to provide not only equal but excellent education for black as well as white, to win the confidence of young people and bring home their alienated elders. The President must persuade a solid majority of the people to support his measures—a majority large enough and firm enough to persuade the Congress to act and the "Establishment" to concur and cooperate.

For only the Establishment can bring about the necessary reforms. It will not be destroyed by activists no matter how loud or profanely they shout or how many banks they burn or laboratories they bomb. For the Establishment, in fact rather than in revolutionary rhetoric, is no more and no less than the hundreds of thousands of men and women who make the nation's decisions, great and small. Without positive leadership the Establishment will continue to be uncertain and divided against itself. Only the President can show the nation's decision makers the way to imperative radical action—and get them to take it. Such a President, however skilled he may be in *presidential politics*, will have to give first priority to the *politics of presidential leadership*—and never be in doubt about the difference. It is because Robert Kennedy well understood the distinction, and because he clearly felt and articulated the imperatives of presidential leadership in the present day, that his campaign of 1968, tragically aborted as it was, can nevertheless provide a valuable kind of case study that may be instructive for today and for tomorrow.

In the course of the 1968 presidential campaign Richard Nixon once observed that "only the President can hold out a vision of the future and rally the people behind it." While the statement revealed a clear perception of the nature of the presidential system and the requirements for effective presidential leadership, it is the irony of his campaign and of his administration that he neither projected such a vision nor, as he hoped to do, took "hold of America" in order to move it forward. Thus he came to the Presidency without any definable mandate except, perhaps, to de-escalate the war in Vietnam. Having failed to win a clear and solid majority in the election, he sought to do so as President.

Like John F. Kennedy, who also failed to win a clear and solid majority, President Nixon's first years in the White House were largely devoted to continuing his campaign in the hope that he could ultimately be "elected." Hence his frequent appeals to the "silent majority," or the "forgotten American." Hence also his appeal to the white South, his stress on law and order, and his steady reassurance to the fearful of the cities, those who have just risen precariously above the poverty line, and to the affluent of the suburbs.[2] By such means he worked to establish a new coalition of what Joseph Kraft has called "Middle Americans" which would keep himself and the Republican party in power by replacing the shattered Democratic coalition of trade union workers, blacks, liberals, intellectuals, and Southern politicians. Nixon's efforts to diminish American involvement in the Vietnam war by withdrawing troops appealed, of course, across most of the spectrum of American thought and answered a universal hope. Yet even success in this well-calculated political course could not produce a mandate "to move America forward."

Thus the country remained largely stagnant, mostly calm on the surface but boiling below, for lack of "vision" and lack of precisely the "activist" leadership President Nixon talked of in his campaign. As James Reston put it:

At the end of his first year, the President must know that he has dealt more effectively with the politics of his problems than he has dealt with the problems themselves. He has dealt with the opponents of the war, but not with the war. He has dealt with the Democratic Party, but not with the young intellectuals, the poor and the blacks.[3]

By the middle of Nixon's term the picture was essentially unchanged. The firing of a liberal cabinet member, repeated attempts to put an anti-integrationist on the Supreme Court, and intemperate campaigning against Democratic congressional candidates produced neither national leadership nor political success.

From this perspective the unfinished 1968 campaign of Robert Kennedy takes on special, critical significance. The tragedy and the pathos of Kennedy's assassination have tended to obscure the meaning of that campaign. That his death would elevate him with his brother to a kind of legendary pinnacle was no doubt inevitable. But it is not enough, in *The New Yorker*'s words, "to remember simply that once a most decent man was here, touching the lives of other people with hope and possibilities and generosity and love."[4] The point is to remember what he was trying to do, for he was acting upon a conception of the Presidency which is of vital consequence no matter who the candidates are in any election, and no matter who is elected.

Robert Kennedy's campaign for the Presidency was essentially a strong, urgent, and persistent call for drastic—even radical—measures, initiated and led by the President, in the major fields of public concern: foreign policy in general and the Vietnam war in particular, poverty, the cities, race relations, alienation of youth, and the problem of public order. Because he sought reconciliation of disheartened and fearful people by a sharp attack on the causes of their discontent, he risked the charge that he was dividing the people. Because its thrust was radical, his campaign was also radically different from the campaigns of the other candidates. Even a hasty reminder of those other campaigns reveals the differences.

The historic importance of Eugene McCarthy's campaign was no doubt his demonstration that an incumbent President seeking renomination may be vulnerable if his policy is deeply and widely unpopular. Whether Lyndon Johnson would have withdrawn after the New Hampshire primary, where McCarthy made his most spectacular showing, or only determined to do so when Robert Kennedy declared his candidacy, or never intended to run again in any case, as he asserted in 1969, there is no doubt that McCarthy rallied the antiwar movement and proved its political potency. Follow-up studies by the Michigan Survey Research Center show that much of McCarthy's New Hampshire vote was simply anti-Johnson and included "hawks" and even people who were not sure how the candidate stood on the war. Nevertheless, peace leaders and an emerging national majority of voters searching for an end to the war were enormously encouraged by the size of McCarthy's vote.

But McCarthy remained a one-issue candidate. His sense of the problems of the poor, the cities, and the blacks, whatever it may have been, was never translated into effective proposals for dealing with them. His appeal, for various reasons, was limited chiefly to the well-educated, whom he courted, and the "concerned" affluent of the universities and the suburbs. He seemed uncertain in the presence of people demanding to know how he proposed to deal with urban decay, or the black ghettoes, or poverty anywhere. He avoided the ghettoes almost entirely. While he issued position papers to display his concern, he never spelled out their application in his speeches.

After the primaries in Oregon, where he won, and California, where he was decisively defeated by Kennedy, McCarthy boasted that he could get the votes "no other Democratic candidate" could get. He was right. In Oregon the normal elements of Kennedy support, the blacks and the poor, were in abnormal minority. Indeed, except in 1964 the state had long been safely Republican. In California

McCarthy again was strong in areas where the minorities were weak. But his successful appeal to the more affluent and conservative, ironically, was his fatal weakness as a Democratic candidate. Because he seemed to foreshadow no serious attack on the status quo, no real threat to the Establishment, he appeared to many as a safe candidate. A vote for McCarthy would express protest against the war and, perhaps, annoyance with Kennedy and dislike of both President Johnson and Richard Nixon. But the consequences would not be unsettling. At the same time, many young people, otherwise tending toward radical concern for the state of the nation and cynical about the Establishment, were satisfied to concentrate on ending the war. Thus McCarthy built a coalition of opposites which might conceivably have elected him, but could not have nominated him. He was, in effect, running against his party.

Paradoxically, McCarthy was also, as Arthur Schlesinger, Jr. put it, "running against the Presidency."[5] It was a continuing theme in his attack on Johnson that too much power had been centered in the President. What was needed, he said, was "not so much . . . leadership," but that the next President should "be prepared to be a kind of channel" where the currents of opinion could flow. To an unspecified degree he would "decentralize" the powers of the Presidency. But to weaken his powers would be to diminish precisely that ability of the President to lead a radical attack on critical problems, which is the paramount advantage of the presidential system. The entire history of the United States shows that Congress not only will not, but cannot, mount such an attack of its own motion. And there is no further alternative. Richard Nixon, Nelson Rockefeller, and Hubert Humphrey at least understood this central fact of American political life. It was the core of Kennedy's campaign. What is regrettable is that after Kennedy's death neither Humphrey nor Nixon proved able or willing to project a radical program and rally a majority behind it. And Rockefeller, who might have done both, entered the Republican contest only after it had been decided.

Hubert Humphrey, whose nomination became a certainty with the death of Kennedy, suffered under two insurmountable handicaps: he could not escape sharing responsibility for the unpopular war, and he had talked too much and too long. Out of loyalty, if not out of conviction, Humphrey valiantly defended President Johnson's policies while asserting at the same time that he himself could bring the war to an honorable end. Since Nixon had supported the war for years, he could only offer a new administration which, he argued, would have a better chance to end it than would Humphrey. In any case, neither candidate was "electable."

With the war issue largely a standoff, Humphrey's long-established image cost him the election. It was commonplace to speak of him as "old hat," even though he never wore one. He was identified with all of the liberal causes for which the Democrats had fought under Harry Truman, Adlai Stevenson, and John Kennedy; and his own contribution had been great, especially in the field of civil rights. But he proposed no new departures. His speeches, almost regardless of what he was saying, sounded precisely like the speeches he had been making for twenty years. To a great extent they were the same.

The trouble was that the Democratic policies and programs, from Franklin Roosevelt to John Kennedy, had largely succeeded and belonged to the past. Trade union power, social security, nearly full employment, public housing, and government assistance to the disadvantaged were all taken for granted. Even the civil rights movement had nearly achieved its goals of political equality for blacks and the outlawing of discrimination. Humphrey seemed to offer only more of the same, at a time when the welfare system was a scandal, the cities needed not simply more housing but reconstruction, a core of permanently unemployed had developed, and the blacks were exercising their political rights in an imperious call for an end to social and economic inequities. Under such conditions Hubert Humphrey's "politics of joy" was a poor joke to too many people.

Richard Nixon's narrow advantage, ironically, was his defeats in 1960 and 1962. They had kept him away from the center of public attention for several years and enabled him, when he returned, to present himself as a changed man who had learned humility and wisdom. He had not talked too much or too long, so that when he spoke he commanded better attention than could Humphrey. That he might end the war seemed possible; that he would restore "law and order" to crime-ridden cities was a welcome promise; that he would "halt" inflation was a fervent hope. He was careful to offer no program for accomplishing any of these cherished goals and thus may well have neutralized some of the animosity he had built up over many years as a sharp-tongued partisan.

In any case, Nixon's campaign was pitched at the same level of abstraction as Humphrey's. The issues thus became secondary. What were at issue were the personalities and public careers of the two candidates. In the end the election was a standoff. Neither could come close to a majority, and a third party candidate, George Wallace, appealing frankly to the fears of the comfortable, won 14 percent of the vote, the highest percentage for a third party candidate in forty-four years.

On any showing, the campaign of 1968 after the national conventions was a disaster. No candidate was to any important degree a popular figure. Despite the millions of words on television, radio, billboards, the printed page, and spoken by the candidates in person to their audiences, little was said that was directly addressed to the needs of the country. There is no way of knowing whether this was because the major candidates were unsure or unimaginative, whether they simply preferred to seek power without specific commitment, or whether, to a degree, partisan and divisive edges were deliberately dulled because the risks of sharpness had been revealed by Kennedy's murder.*

What is certain is that the issues were blurred and that their blurring was a consequence of Robert Kennedy's death. At the least, he would himself have kept them sharp.

---

* Governor Rockefeller told the National Press Club a few days after Kennedy's death that he "died because he dared to speak out on the issues before the American people."

This, to use his favorite word, was the nation's "unacceptable" loss, more even than the loss of an attractive and courageous man.

In 1968 the United States was still paying the heavy cost of the politics of inaction which President Eisenhower had successfully practiced in the 1950s. That Eisenhower was one of the most popular of all American Presidents was demonstrated beyond dispute by his two victories over Adlai Stevenson and by the opinion polls of 1960 which showed that had he been eligible for a third term he could easily have defeated any Democratic candidate. Though a certain measure of stability, and widespread euphoria, was undoubtedly encouraged by his policy of holding himself above some conflicts and skillfully blurring others, Eisenhower could not hold up or even significantly moderate the increasing rate of change. He could appeal to sharply diverse groups at so lofty a level as to hold their confidence in himself while they sought other scapegoats for their grievances, but he could not effectively address the causes of grievance. While Eisenhower's popularity spread across the spectrum of opinion and interest—indeed, partly *because* it did so—he could not move to close the growing gap between the improverished minority and the affluent majority, nor could he adopt and press for a program to halt the decay of the cities and reconstruct urban life in America. Above all, by holding himself aloof from the conflict over civil rights, refusing even to comment on the desegregation decisions of the Supreme Court, he allowed the conflict to be exacerbated for lack of moral leadership at the seat of national power.

Because peace was universally desired in 1953, Eisenhower could and did seek to negotiate a truce in Korea. His efforts certainly enhanced his popularity. But his dramatic trip to Korea after his election in November 1952 was no more than a popular gesture. When armistice came in July 1953, it was owing less to any acts of leadership by the American President than to the death of Stalin and to concessions to the Chinese on the issue of interviewing prisoners of war—concessions previously refused by the Truman administration. Indeed, almost the only substantial monuments to Eisenhower's administration were the International Atomic Energy Agency, for which history may one day grant him a cherished place, and the National Highway System, both of which were essentially noncontroversial.[6]

The consequence of Eisenhower's popular success was a heavy heritage for John F. Kennedy: provocations by Russian leadership to test how much the United States had been weakened, deterioration of the cities, a nearly rigid wall between the affluent and the excluded, and critically heightened racial tensions over elementary civil rights.

In the 1960 campaign Richard Nixon necessarily stood on the Eisenhower record, while Kennedy frequently asserted the need for a strong President. "In the challenging, revolutionary Sixties," he said, "the American Presidency will demand more than ringing manifestoes issued from the rear of the battle. It will demand that the President place himself in the very thick of the fight, that he care passionately about the fate of the people he heads, that he be willing to serve them at the risk of incurring their momentary displeasure."[7] He was prepared, in short, to do what needed to be done and what his predecessor had failed to do. In his campaign he proposed a number of concrete measures—executive action on civil rights under existing law, measures to provide more jobs by increasing the economic growth rate, and federal aid to public schools. He would, he said, "get this country moving again."

But viewed in his own terms John Kennedy's campaign was a failure. He could not persuade a clear majority to give him the mandate he sought. He was elected by a plurality with less than a 1 percent margin over his opponent. Nixon, in fact, carried more states than did Kennedy and lost only because Kennedy won enough of the more heavily populated states to put together an electoral majority. The chief reasons for the approximate dead heat in the popular vote were no doubt the lingering euphoria of the Eisenhower years, with which Nixon was to a degree identified, and Kennedy's Catholicism. Opinion polls showed that other, non-Catholic, Democratic candidates might have won by substantial margins, probably because Nixon was not personally popular enough to hold the Eisenhower majority together.

For whatever reasons one chooses to assign, the historic fact was that John Kennedy entered the Presidency with a well-defined program but no mandate to carry it out, and with control of Congress in the hands of a perennial coalition of conservatives opposed to the extension of civil rights and to precisely the sort of experimentation in social and economic policy Kennedy advocated.

Under these circumstances, Kennedy decided to devote his energies to action in the field of foreign policy and to an educational campaign on domestic issues. He inaugurated the Peace Corps, jousted with Khrushchev over Berlin and Cuba, pressed for settlement in Laos, and by establishing the Alliance for Progress made a new approach to Latin America. Meanwhile he used his press conferences and well-publicized speaking appearances to explain the "new economics," to advocate aid to the public schools while guarding against attack on his Catholic flank by opposing aid to parochial schools, to plead for liberal immigration laws, and to press the case for a new attack on the problems of the cities. In effect, he was continuing his election campaign, seeking to win while in office the majority he had not won as a candidate.

Candidate Kennedy had laid it down that "no President . . . can escape politics." As President he practiced what he preached. In order to maintain as cordial relations as possible with Southern Democrats whose votes he needed on economic measures, not only did he not ask for civil rights legislation, he even dismayed his most devoted supporters by putting off for almost two years the executive action on segregated housing he had promised in his campaign. On the other hand, he delighted the same followers and risked the wrath of the business community, and some conservative congressmen, by exerting unprecedented presidential pressure on the steel industry to prevent a rise in prices, a popular anti-inflation gesture. Other, less noted political activity was equally calculated to increase his popular support. And he succeeded.

By the time he had been in office for two years, the polls consistently demonstrated that President Kennedy had eliminated residual fears of his Catholicism and won the approval of majorities rising at times to over 80 percent and seldom falling below 65 percent. There was a continuing gap between the approval he commanded personally and the support the polls showed he could muster for his program. But support for the program also steadily increased.

In the off-year congressional elections of 1962, in which Kennedy was an active campaigner, the Democrats held even in the House and gained two seats in the Senate, a significant achievement in view of the normal expectation that the party in power will lose strength in the off years. Thereafter, with the presidential campaign of 1964 for practical purposes already under way, Kennedy began to assume in full the character of popular partisan leader he had advocated and been preparing for. Civil rights was the issue he chose to signal his new approach to power.

Perhaps it would be more accurate to say that it was civil rights that chose him. His promised executive order requiring integration of federally assisted housing probably helped some northern congressmen to hold their seats in the 1962 election, but it had little or no meaning to blacks who were fighting discrimination in schools, buses, and all sorts of public places. The Black Revolution was on. Violence arising out of sit-ins and demonstrations, bombings in Birmingham, and the bitter tension over the integration of universities in Mississippi and Alabama forced the President's hand. Robert Kennedy, struggling, as Attorney General, to exert the last bit of leverage out of existing law and presidential authority, declared emphatically that regardless of the political risks radical and sweeping legislation could be put off no longer. The President agreed and took the problem to the country.

John Kennedy's advocacy of civil rights legislation in the spring and summer of 1963 was steady and powerful. Predictably, his popularity, by the barometer of the polls, fell sharply. But it remained around the 60-percent mark, solid enough to give confidence that at last he had the mandate he had always been seeking. The Kennedy of 1963 was a very different President from the Kennedy of 1961. He was now fighting for a program—civil rights, housing, a war on poverty, radical revision of immigration policies—urging Congress to act, and openly laying the groundwork for a 1964 campaign to win public support for measures the Congress emasculated, put off, or refused to pass. At the moment of his assassination Kennedy was vigorously practicing his own precepts for strong presidential leadership.

As President, Lyndon Johnson began with the handicap that he could not hope to match the personal popularity of his predecessor. But he could and did capitalize on the national mood of sympathy and renewed resolve that followed the assassination. And he fully shared Kennedy's views of the presidential office. He had been initiated into the politics of national leadership by Franklin Roosevelt. As Majority Leader of the Senate he had shown both a liking and a capacity for tough political infighting always accompanied by appeals to "reasonableness."

What was new about Johnson as President was his strongly partisan liberalism. His metamorphosis should not have been surprising. As a young congressman in the 1930s he had been a devoted supporter of the New Deal and was a favorite of Roosevelt. His own roots were in Texas regional Populism rather than Texas Bourbonism. It was only as a senator in the 1950s, dependent on statewide support, that he often seemed to compromise out of all effectiveness the liberal programs favored by the majority of his party. He seldom tangled with the Southern veterans and normally stood with them on matters vital to his own security as a senator from Texas. But when he saw opportunities for national leadership he had not hesitated to push and pull the Senate.

By 1957 Johnson had been persuaded that congressional legislation on civil rights was both necessary and politically feasible. In that year he engineered the first civil rights law since Reconstruction—a weak measure certainly, but nevertheless, as he well knew, the beginning of a new era. Given his leaning toward use of the national power to help the unfortunate and his grasp of the necessities in the drive for civil rights, it was entirely predictable that Johnson, emancipated from his Texas constituency, would be a strong, partisan, and liberal President.

While the national economy had begun to revive under the policies of President Kennedy, deterioration in the cities had not been halted nor had the poverty gap been appreciably narrowed during the years when he sought to establish his leadership. And racial tension had heightened to an ugly pitch, despite the growing confidence of blacks in both John and Robert Kennedy. Johnson moved immediately and skillfully to bring the great influence of the Presidency to bear on the Congress and to reassure the people as he pushed for adoption of the Kennedy program and added significant measures of his own. Before the Kennedy-Johnson term ended Congress gave the President what he asked in civil rights and the beginnings of a program to fight poverty.

Johnson's election in 1964 to a term in his own right was ambiguous in some ways and paradoxical in others. In a contest between two men neither of whom could boast of wide personal popularity, Johnson defeated Barry Goldwater by the greatest margin since 1936. He campaigned forthrightly for federal aid to education, for a war on poverty, and for extension of civil rights laws to cover voting. Not only his own victory but the immense Democratic margin in the congressional election proved his mandate to lead and act in these fields.

But Johnson campaigned with equal emphasis as a peace candidate, a man who could be trusted to keep the United States from deep involvement in the Vietnam war. He would not, he asserted repeatedly, "send American boys" to do what "Asian boys should do." Goldwater, a somewhat extravagant anti-Communist, advocated strong American measures, including use of bombers piloted by Americans, not only to protect the government of South Vietnam but to defeat their Communist-led opponents. In a rash moment he even suggested the possibility of using small nuclear weapons as defoliants to deny the insurgents their customary jungle cover. Johnson, and other Democratic campaigners, were quick to label Goldwater as irresponsible in foreign affairs, a man who could not be trusted to hold and use wisely the great powers of the Presidency, which include control of nuclear weapons. Thus it was fair to say that Johnson won a clear mandate to keep the United States out of the Vietnam war. The United States had been providing military supplies to the Saigon government for years, and had committed some few thousand soldiers as advisers and helicopter pilots. Johnson won solid support for keeping American assistance at this low level, avoiding intervention with combat soldiers in the air or on the ground. Like Wilson in 1916, "he had kept us out of the war" and seemed to promise he would continue to do so.

In 1964, for the first time since the election of 1938 had restored their power, the coalition of southern conservative Democrats and northern and western conservative Republicans lost control of both houses of Congress. The new liberal, pro-Johnson majorities, expertly led by the President himself, quickly put through massive federal aid to education, established and funded an Office of Economic Opportunity, approved an amendment to the Constitution forbidding discriminatory practices in federal elections, passed a voting rights law to apply the same principles in the states, and passed other measures to bring into being what Johnson liked to call the "Great Society."

If Lyndon Johnson's administration were to be judged on the President's performance between November 22, 1963 and the summer of 1965, the verdict, from whatever point of vantage, would have been very different from what it was when he left office on January 20, 1969. In those first two years Johnson led a big majority of the country and of the Congress toward goals of his own and John Kennedy's choosing, brilliantly projecting a politics of consensus ("let us reason together for the common good") to achieve a program at once partisan and divisive. But partisanship was minimized and division diminished to scarcely audible voices because the President's programs were so broadly appealing to the mass of the people. In a sense Johnson himself rode the crest of the wave of the popularity of his policies and programs. In some ways his first two years like the early years of the New Deal were a watershed in American history. In any event, whether one approved or disapproved the directions in which the country was moving, it was clear that the presidential system was working effectively in the hands of a strong President.

In the light of what might have been, President Johnson's decision to intervene in the Vietnam war seems doubly tragic. Not only did intervention fail to win the war itself, but it fatally stunted the growth of the Great Society before even its outlines could be fully sketched. And not the least serious consequence was a growing uneasiness about the Presidency itself.

The war was not immediately unpopular. Indeed, opinion polls showed substantial support for Johnson's policy almost continuously until the disaster of the Tet season in 1968. But there was a growing doubt, underlined by the opposition of some leading senators and by the disquieting tendency of the government, including the President, to speak with something less than candor of the news from Vietnam and of the magnitude and degree of United States involvement. It was during this period that Robert Kennedy, as we shall see in the next chapter, reassessing his position on the war, gradually became the national symbol of opposition and began to appear as a possible alternative to President Johnson for the Democratic nomination in 1968.

But whatever the state of opinion about the war, some things were beyond dispute. The war drained massive resources away from possible application to domestic needs. As the cost of the war increased, reaching $30 billion or more a year, appropriations for Great Society programs and agencies were inevitably cut back. At the same time many, if not most, of the more able and imaginative leaders among the blacks, in the war on poverty, and in the effort to rehabilitate the cities became discouraged and even rebellious.

The ghettoes of the cities were aflame with arson, riot, and pillage. The Peace Corps, once a dramatic expression of youthful idealism, became an escape hatch from the draft. Growing numbers of young men not only protested the war but refused to serve. The generation gap, once scarcely more than the theme of the hippies, the New Left, and the older alarmists, came into focus as a profound alienation of very large numbers of young people not only from the war but from what they called the "Establishment" and the "system."

As President Johnson steadily lost popular favor and his influence over Congress diminished, he gave less and less attention to the domestic programs he had launched and became not only preoccupied but ultimately almost obsessed by the war. So did a great many citizens, young and old. Under such circumstances it was not surprising that growing numbers of people looked to Robert Kennedy as a symbol of what might be—a way to restore the national spirit to the "burden and the glory" of the John Kennedy years. Those years, indeed, looked more and more glorious as they retreated in time, more glorious than in fact they had ever been. It was a time when far more people claimed to have voted for the assassinated President than had in fact done so. And the turning toward his brother was certainly inspired at first more by sentiment and nostalgia than by any clear notion of what sort of man he was or how he would lead the nation were he to become President. It was Kennedy's historic role to replace Lyndon Johnson in the minds of liberals, intellectuals, young people, blacks, and the poor in general as a potential strong President who could end the war and lead a successful radical attack on the domestic crisis. But the transformation was gradual and painful and full of hesitation.

Kennedy's own response to the outreaching of people toward him was for a long time uncertain. He knew that the feeling for himself was largely a reflex of emotion among people mourning his brother. When he stood before the Democratic National Convention of 1964 to receive perhaps the most sustained and moving ovation ever accorded anyone at a party convention, his own tears were plain to see. There was never any doubt that he would try to carry on where his brother had left off, but there were many doubts as to how to do it. He could act only through the Democratic party. But that party was now in the hands of another man who was President of the United States. Any sort of challenge to him would seem to reveal in Kennedy little but naked ambition. Johnson had decided against asking Kennedy to run with him as vice-presidential candidate. He could not continue as Attorney General in the cabinet of a man who disliked him and rightly saw in him a potential rival. And so he chose, for lack of a better option and without enthusiasm, an opportunity to run in New York for the Senate.

Robert Kennedy's campaign for the Senate in 1964 offers only a few clues to the sort of leadership he would be displaying by 1968. The issues between himself and his opponent, Senator Kenneth Keating, were muted because both men were liberals and because Keating made a bipartisan appeal by refusing to support the Republican presidential candidate, Barry Goldwater. Keating ran on his record as a senator; Kennedy, handicapped by the cry of "carpetbagger," ran on the record of the Kennedy-Johnson administration in which he had been a central figure for three-and-a-half years. The differences thus generated were sometimes heatedly presented by the candidates but usually lacked compelling substance.

What differentiated Kennedy's campaign; and won him the election, was has style and his special appeal to the blacks, the Puerto Ricans, and the poor of every description. Diffident at first, and uncomfortable with excited crowds, Kennedy learned to capitalize on his name, his winsome manner, and his youth. As people reached out to touch him he began to reach back. The crowds gave him confidence and stirred in him an enthusiasm for the campaign that was contagious. As the days went by he relied less and less on prepared speeches, contenting himself and his audiences with short, sharp thrusts at the opposition, forthright demands for "doing better," and skillful use of moving quotations. "To seek a newer world" became his motto in the course of the campaign and remained a frequent expression of his appeal to the spirit of progress and adventure. If the young candidate was in fact anything but an elderly Ulysses yearning for one last moment of discovery, Tennyson's words nevertheless suited Kennedy well enough:

> The lights begin to twinkle from the rocks:
> The long day wanes: the slow moon climbs: the deep
> Moans round with many voices. Come, my friends,
> 'Tis not too late to seek a newer world.

As his personal style developed, his sense of identification with the needs and hopes of people developed with it. It was in Brooklyn's Bedford-Stuyvesant and in Harlem, and in the slums of upstate cities like Buffalo and Rochester that Robert Kennedy first came to feel the bitterness and the yearning of those who did not "belong" to the affluent society. Reversing the normal progression, as he sought their votes he gradually became their spokesman, and as their spokesman he began to search for solutions to the critical problems, not only of New York but of the whole country, problems of poverty, racial discrimination, and alienation. In 1964 he promised that as a senator he would propose legislation "to break the tragic pattern of decayed neighborhoods, slums, and poverty," and to provide decent housing and expanded opportunities for stable jobs for blacks and others discarded in the wake of technology.[8] The search for ways to carry out these promises became, after the campaign of 1964, the preoccupation of his life. The results of that search, in experimental projects already begun and in concrete proposals for national action, formed the basis of his campaign for the Presidency in 1968.

In the campaign of 1964 Kennedy gave vigorous support to President Johnson, including his Vietnam policy. The President was pledged to carry out the program of John Kennedy for domestic reforms and was promising to keep the United States involvement in Vietnam at the level of assistance only, while the Republican candidate seemed to suggest more drastic measures that might well put the United States directly into the war. Robert Kennedy not only had no real political choice, as a Democratic candidate for the Senate, but felt no principled objection to wholehearted support of the national Democratic ticket of Johnson and Hubert Humphrey.

As he moved toward a decisive victory over Senator Keating, Kennedy's immediate concerns were not how or when to try for the Presidency. A presidential campaign in 1972 was too remote to think about. At the University of Rochester, when some students charged him with running for the Senate in New York only as a stepping stone to the Presidency, he answered at first with quips and then more seriously:

Let's assume that I want to be President of the United States. In the first place, truthfully now—I can't go any place in 1968. We've got President Lyndon Johnson—and I think he's going to be re-elected in 1968. Now we get to 1972. That's eight years. Assuming that I am still using it [the Senate seat] as a power base, I'm going to have to be re-elected in six years.

If I'm re-elected—if I have done such an outstanding job and I really want to be President, I'm going to have to do a tremendous job for the State of New York, for the people of the State of New York . . . . Then if I have done such an outstanding job in eight years that people demand all over the country that I be a presidential candidate, I don't see how New York suffers.[9]

But he had scarcely taken his seat in the Senate when such "demands" began to be heard. And President Johnson's changing policy toward the Vietnam war soon raised disturbing questions in Kennedy's mind.

TWO

Vietnam and the Directions of Foreign Policy

By the winter of 1968 it was already clear that no presidential candidate, except perhaps President Johnson himself, would propose to continue the war in Vietnam, or even to support it wholeheartedly. And Johnson had always insisted that peace "with honor," not military victory, was his overriding purpose. The national temper, "hawkish" in 1965, had shifted many degrees. By 1968 it was "dovish." While a slight majority, according to the polls, still thought the American intervention had been right, a far larger majority now favored seeking a negotiated peace. There was a substantial majority for stopping the bombing of North Vietnam.

There were many contributing reasons for the change. The war was dragging on. American boys were being killed or wounded for purposes not clearly understood. And no end was in sight, despite the steady stream of optimistic statements from the Pentagon. Support for President Johnson and the war effort dropped sharply with the Tet days of 1968, when a massive Communist-led offensive unexpectedly struck almost every city and sizable village in South Vietnam. The United States Embassy in Saigon was directly attacked, a painful symbolic defeat for the Americans, and Hue, the second most important city of the country, was captured and held for some days. The Americans and their South Vietnamese allies recovered, of course, and presently drove back their opponents at every point, inflicting incredibly high casualties. But many Americans simply could not accept the official announcement that the Tet battle had been a "victory" over the Communists.

23

As the war seemed to go badly, the mounting criticism of American intervention by American critics, to say nothing of foreign critics and governments, seemed to be vindicated. Some senators, like Wayne Morse and J. William Fulbright, had from the first opposed President Johnson's dispatch of ground forces and bombing planes. But neither was a political leader with an important national following. And though many well-known political and intellectual figures joined the "peace movement," their impact was minimal until Robert Kennedy placed himself, in effect, at the head of the President's opposition. More than any other one person, Kennedy was responsible for the massive shift in opinion that had made itself felt by the beginning of 1968 and was so dramatically demonstrated by Senator Eugene McCarthy's strong showing in the New Hampshire Democratic presidential primary.

For Kennedy it was a long and tortured time from the days when he shared with his brother the hope that American military equipment and advice, together with economic and technical assistance, would enable the South Vietnamese to mount an effective counterinsurgency, to the summer of 1965 when he came to the reluctant conviction that, whatever might have been, the facts were that intervention was a confession of failure and that the war must be brought to an end.

The case of Vietnam was important from the outset to the Kennedy administration, not only because President Eisenhower had committed the United States to support the government in Saigon, but also because the war then developing was basically an insurgency, led by Communists but involving many non-Communists. The war posed new questions as to what kind of assistance would be practical and effective. John Kennedy had for years criticized President Eisenhower and Secretary of State John Foster Dulles for relying almost exclusively on weapons of mass destruction both for American security and for the United States' contribution to peacekeeping. As President, Kennedy was anxious to develop a versatile capability that would enable the United States not only to meet the more remote threat of nuclear war but to act effectively in so-called brush-fire wars.

The threat of the world Communist movement had already altered in character, after the Korean War, from the possibility of massive invasions across national boundaries to ceaseless probings for opportunities to overthrow weak or infant governments from within. The model was no longer the revolution and civil war in Russia but the Chinese success against Chiang Kai-shek's Nationalists. In Cuba, the Philippines, Burma, Indonesia, Malaya, Laos, and Vietnam itself insurgency had been led by Communists practicing, sometimes quite literally, the precepts of Mao Tse-tung. The new administration recognized that nuclear weapons were useless as means for countering indigenous insurgent campaigns. Experience in Malaya and the Philippines showed that such problems were essentially political, not military. Vietnam should be a kind of proving ground for new strategies and new tactics.

Robert Kennedy, as his brother's closest adviser and a member of the National Security Council, shared fully the President's views on Vietnam. In October 1962, for example, he told an American Legion convention that Americans were serving in Vietnam

. . . because last November a comprehensive program was initiated calling for many forms of American aid to reverse the trend in South Vietnam. This included military assistance to the friendly forces combatting the Communists, economic assistance to the villagers who were the Communists' principal targets, and administrative and technical assistance to bolster the Vietnam government. . . . this kind of warfare can be long, drawn out and costly, but if Communism is to be stopped, it is necessary. And we mean to see this job through to the finish.[1]

Believing that an effective program of assistance would be sufficient, he did not, however, mean that the United States had accepted or should accept an obligation to fight the war.

In the councils of the White House, and of the Pentagon under Secretary of Defense Robert McNamara, intensive studies of insurgency and the means of countering it were under way. The advice of experienced experts was sought and heeded. Sir Robert Thompson, British designer of the strategy that had succeeded in Malaya, and General Edward Lansdale, a major figure in the defeat of the Huk insurgency in the Philippines, were called in as consultants. American soldiers were trained in techniques of defeating guerrillas at their own specialty of jungle warfare. And Green Berets were sent to Vietnam to advise and teach South Vietnamese soldiers how to operate not only in the jungles but behind enemy lines. At the same time President Diem was urged to emphasize police protection of the villages and, where the insurgent threat could not be contained, to move the population to new, well-defended "strategic hamlets." Roads were to be improved, schools and health centers built in the countryside, official corruption rooted out, and above all, land tenure practices and laws were to be radically revised to rid the farmers of the incubus of absentee landlordism.

All this, as Robert Kennedy said, would take a long time. Sir Robert Thompson, whose strategy in Malaya had needed twelve years to eliminate Communist insurgency, estimated that it would take even longer in Vietnam.[2] Perhaps it was precisely the prospect of such "long, drawn out warfare" that made the Thompson-Lansdale strategy unpalatable to many planners in the Pentagon, and finally unacceptable to the Joint Chiefs of Staff. For its part, the Saigon government had no enthusiasm for a strategy of counterinsurgency which proposed, in effect, that the government itself make almost the same revolution the Communists advocated, thus overturning precisely the privileged elite on which the government rested. In any case, it is certain that the effort was abortive, and the military situation steadily deteriorated.

As both Arthur Schlesinger, Jr. and Theodore Sorenson have said, President Kennedy, at the time of his death, had not made a firm decision as to how far the United States should go in the effort to shore up the Saigon government, either before or after the assassination of President Diem. However, evidence revealed in 1970 by Kenneth O'Donnell and Senator Mike Mansfield seems to indicate that the President had reached a firm decision to withdraw military as distinct from logistical or economic support.[3]

But when Lyndon Johnson succeeded to the Presidency, it was predictable that American measures would be escalated to the level the military leadership might think necessary. As early as 1962 Vice President Johnson had returned from a trip to Vietnam convinced, as he advised President Kennedy, that the United States should immediately intervene with combat troops. He had recommended that fifty thousand soldiers be sent to Vietnam. One of his first reported statements as President was that he did not intend to be the first American President to lose a war to the Communists.

Nevertheless, it was a long time before President Johnson was persuaded that massive intervention was necessary, and his measured pace of escalation was well calculated politically to hold the support of public opinion. When, in the spring of 1964, he asked the Senate to express their concurrence with his desire to take whatever countermeasures might be necessary to protect American ships in the Gulf of Tonkin, there was no important opposition.

Robert Kennedy, still serving as Attorney General, likewise continued his support of the American policy toward Vietnam. But later in the year, after the bombing had started and he was a candidate for the United States Senate, he appears to have begun to feel uneasy. Differences between his view and that of the President gradually became apparent. Asked at a news conference in October what advice he would give the President on Vietnam he answered: "Well, I've given advice before as to what I think needs to be done. I think that . . . (there) has to be the support of the people for the military effort . . . (and there) has to be support of the people for the government." He emphasized the fact that there had been three coups in Saigon in a year. Such instability was not conducive to popular confidence. "I think that the people have to feel that there is political progress being made and that they can be protected in their communities, protected in their villages, and I think that once there is that confidence, then I think the war will be won."[4]

Like most liberals, Kennedy warmly applauded President Johnson's speech at Johns Hopkins on April 6, 1965. At that moment the President seemed to be shifting from a policy of military defeat of the Viet Cong-North Vietnam enemy to a policy of political settlement. He offered the Communists negotiations without prior conditions, and pledged a billion dollars of American money for rehabilitation of the whole of Vietnam and for multinational development of the Mekong River Valley. But the bombing was nevertheless continued, even intensified, and as the Saigon government appeared on the verge of collapse, the President ordered a massive intervention of American combat soldiers.

By early summer, though still wishing to remain loyal to the President, Kennedy was struggling with a growing belief that American policy had gone seriously wrong. In June he was saying that "military action on our part is essential," but a month later he revealed the causes of his growing doubts: "Victory in a revolutionary war is not won by escalation, but by de-escalation . . . air attacks by a government on its own villages are likely to be far more dangerous and costly to the people than is the individual and selective terrorism of an insurgent movement."[5]

It was six more restive months before Kennedy finally reached his fateful decision to break with the administration. Meanwhile, American intervention was continually escalated in the name of bringing about negotiations, causing doubt to spread around the country and the world as to whether the United States really wished to negotiate at all. Kennedy's own doubts finally became irresistible. In a speech to the Senate on February 19, 1966, he broke cleanly with Johnson. Thereafter he was the leader of the opposition, despite his often repeated statements that he "expected," for reasons of party loyalty, to support President Johnson for reelection in 1968.

Kennedy's position, as he laid it down in the Senate speech, was a logical consequence of the failure of both the

Saigon government and the American military to hold to a strategy of counterinsurgency which would have placed security itself as the principal objective. Instead, a policy of military victory had been adopted that was not working and that Kennedy had always believed could not be made to work.

Military victory requires that we crush both our adversary's strength and his will to continue the battle; that the forces from the North be compelled to withdraw beyond the border; that much of Vietnam be destroyed and its people killed; that we continue to occupy South Vietnam as long as our presence is required to insure that hostilities, including insurgency, will not be resumed. And this will be a very long time indeed. . . . it would mean rapidly increasing commitments of American forces. It would mean a growing risk of widening war—with North Vietnam, with China, even with the Soviet Union. It would lead, indeed already has led, thoughtless people to advocate the use of nuclear weapons. And it would involve all these things—commitment, risk, and spreading destruction—in pursuit of a goal which is at best uncertain, and at worst unattainable.[6]

Kennedy did not entirely rule out such a military victory. "The intransigence of our adversaries," he said, "may leave us no alternative."

It is important to note that Kennedy's attack on military policy was not an attack on anticommunism. He did not then or afterwards question the purposes for which the Americans had gone to the assistance of the South Vietnamese. He did not then or afterwards call for unilateral withdrawal. Thus, though he became the de facto political leader of the "peace movement," he never was "of" that movement. In the campaign of 1968 he was upon occasion to be booed and harshly criticized by young people for this very reason.

What Kennedy did advocate in February 1966 and afterwards until his death was a direct approach to the original enemy in South Vietnam: negotiations with the National Liberation Front leading to a coalition government for South Vietnam.

Whatever the exact status of the National Liberation Front—puppet or partly independent—any negotiated settlement must accept the fact that there are discontented elements in South Vietnam, Communist and non-Communist, who desire to change the existing political and economic system of the country. There are three things you can do with such groups: kill or repress them, turn the country over to them, or admit them to a share of power and responsibility. . . .

The last—to admit them to a share of power and responsibility—is at the heart of the hope for a negotiated settlement.[7]

Kennedy was fully aware of the difficulty of reaching an agreement on such a basis and of the risks involved both for the non-Communist Vietnamese and for the United States. There was, for example, no certainty that social and economic progress under a coalition government would be sufficient to "weaken the appeal of Communism." In holding free elections there was risk that Communist-led elements might take full power, even that North Vietnam would swallow up the South.

But no other sensible solution seemed to him possible. The risks and the uncertainties were worthwhile. In any case, there must be built-in safeguards in the form of "international guarantees to back up the agreement." And there must be "good faith and mutual self-interest."

Because there was no way for him to press such views on Vietnam firmly enough, other than to take them to the public and try to bring massive pressure on the administration, Robert Kennedy became for all practical purposes a candidate for President. No matter how frequently he disclaimed ambition or intent, there had to be a clear implication that he was himself the alternative to an administration which would not shift its policy from military to political efforts to bring about negotiations.

In the fall of 1967 Kennedy wrote a long essay on Vietnam for his book *To Seek a Newer World*. The book itself, though not so labeled by its author until the second edition in April 1968, was the basic document of his campaign for the Presidency. The style and spirit of that campaign were foreshadowed in the foreword to the chapter on Vietnam:

It is appropriate to inject here a note both personal and public. I was involved in many of the early decisions on Vietnam, decisions which helped set us on our present path. It may be that the effort was doomed from the start, that it was never really possible to bring all the people of South Vietnam under the rule of the successive governments we supported—governments, one after another, riddled with corruption, inefficiency, and greed; governments which did not and could not successfully capture and energize the national feeling of their people. If that is the case, as it well may be, then I am willing to bear my share of the responsibility, before history and before my fellow-citizens. But past error is no excuse for its own perpetuation. Tragedy is a tool for the living to gain wisdom, not a guide by which to live.[8]

He concluded his *mea culpa* with an aphorism from the *Antigone* of Sophocles which he often thereafter quoted in campaign speeches: "All men make mistakes, but a good man yields when he knows his course is wrong, and repairs the evil. The only sin is pride."

Like the Senate speech of 1966, Kennedy's campaign statements in 1968 differed from those of his opponents and from the general line of the peace movement precisely because he refused to repudiate the original effort in Vietnam. The massive United States intervention, "these conventional efforts"—bombing, strafing, and sweeping the jungles in search of the enemy—were, he said, taking place "because an earlier struggle failed." That struggle was "the attempt of the Government of South Vietnam, with our aid and assistance, to build a viable government and society and to stem an insurgency that as late as 1959 . . . had an active strength of only three thousand men."[9]

The point, as Kennedy saw it, had never been and should never be merely to stop the spread of communism. His whole approach to foreign policy, not only in Vietnam but elsewhere as we shall see, was predicated on the belief that Communists appealed successfully only to people whose grievances were real. What was needed was an attack on the grievances. No other policy—no matter how intense the bombings, how massive the scale of ground operations, or how terrible the firepower—could in the long run win against the Communists or other insurgents in what Mao called "wars of national liberation."

For if these conflicts are called wars, and have deep international consequences, they are at the same time not wars, and their outcome is determined by internal factors. Their essence is political. They are struggles for the control of government, contests for the allegiance of men. Allegiance is won as in any political contest, by an idea and a faith, by promise and performance. Governments resist such challenges only by being effective and responsive to the needs of their people.

Herein lay the failure of the Saigon government and of American policy. And this was why the war should be stopped as quickly as possible by seeking agreement with the enemy.

Conventional military force and advanced weapons technology are useful only to destroy. But a government cannot make war on its own people, or destroy its own country. Suppose, for example, that a government force is fired upon from a village. A government that attacks that village from the air, or with heavy artillery, abandons all pretense of protecting the people of the village.

This, of course, was exactly what the armies of South Vietnam were doing, as were their American allies.

But such protection is the first duty of any government worthy of the name, and its absence is not ignored by the village. Rather, as General Edward Lansdale has told us, "civilian hatred of the military resulting from such actions is a powerful motive for joining (the insurgents)."

But protection, Kennedy insisted, was not the only inescapable obligation of government to its citizens.

Guns and bombs cannot fill empty stomachs or educate children, cannot build homes or heal the sick. But these are the ends for which men establish and obey governments; they will give their allegiance only to governments that meet these needs.[10]

He often cited the case of the Philippines, where a losing battle with Huk insurgents was turned into a decisive victory by the reform leadership of Ramon Magsaysay. Without such leadership and dedication, there was no hope in Vietnam; and there was no such leadership or dedication. "Foreign assistance," said Kennedy, "can reinforce a national will, but foreign intervention cannot provide a substitute where a national will is lacking."[11]

In the light of his own share in the initial effort to shore up South Vietnam, his regrets at failure were often poignant. But the thrust of his speeches and writings was always toward learning the lessons and "doing better." One lesson was to avoid making commitments to beleaguered governments without insisting that they make the necessary reforms. "Our efforts [in Vietnam]," he wrote, "were grounded not only in a realistic knowledge that the struggle must otherwise be unsuccessful, but also in the nature of our commitment: to the South Vietnamese people as a whole, rather than any narrow element."[12] What had happened by the later 1960s was that the United States had tied itself to precisely such a "narrow element" and was in effect making war against the people of Vietnam. This was intolerable. It betrayed the whole original purpose and intent of American policy.

Another lesson to be learned was that the effort to compensate for failure by massive military measures would have disastrous consequences elsewhere, too. "I found in Europe," he wrote, "among men and nations who wish only good for the United States, deep anxiety and fundamental disagreement with our policy; we were, they felt, becoming dangerously irrelevant."[13] In other regions, the consequences of American policy might be even more serious: ". . . in the Near East, Latin America, and Africa, the diversion of our attention, resources, and energies has seriously limited our capacity to affect the course of events, and protect far more important national interests." He went on to cite the case of India, "one of the truly important areas of the world," suffering from hunger and facing endless internal crisis "in large part for want of development capital," while the United States was spending thirty billion dollars a year on the Vietnam war.[14]

But the unhappy consequences of President Johnson's Vietnam policy were not confined to limiting American capabilities to act abroad. The war was "also diverting resources that might have been used to help eliminate American poverty, improve the education of our children, enhance the quality of our national life—perhaps even to save the nation from internal violence and chaos."[15]

His essay on Vietnam provided Robert Kennedy as a candidate for President with most of the basic material for his speeches on the war. But the purposes of the campaign, of course, were different. And so the speeches were more pointed, the language sometimes stronger, and the appeal for personal support a continuing theme. The emphasis in 1968 was on action, on what could be done.

In the first days of his candidacy, he belabored administration policy with the bitter words of Tacitus on the barbarians at Rome: "They made a desert and called it peace." After President Johnson, on March 30, announced a partial halt to the bombing, a renewed effort to get to the negotiating table, and his own withdrawal from the presidential contest, Kennedy softened his tone.

But the need to alter his campaign tactics meant no change in his views on the war. While he denounced the slaughter of Vietnamese by Americans as immoral, he as vigorously berated the other side. "Let us have no misunderstanding," he told the students at Kansas State University, "the Viet Cong are a brutal enemy indeed. Time and time again they have shown their willingness to sacrifice innocent civilians, to engage in torture and murder and despicable terror to achieve their ends." There could, he said, "be no easy moral answer to this war."[16] Statements like these cost Kennedy a good deal of his popularity among the young people who had for years shouted, sometimes even screamed enthusiasm for him. Many university students, drawn to McCarthy because he had challenged Johnson first, now sharply criticized Kennedy for balancing his attack on Vietnam policy with insistence on the complexity of the war and the brutality of the Communists. Young people brandishing Viet Cong flags booed Kennedy and taunted him, but they did not budge him. At McCarthy rallies they could and did feel at home; at Kennedy rallies they were uncomfortable.

At Kansas State in March and thereafter at many colleges and universities, as well as on street corners, in public squares and auditoriums, Kennedy stuck to his theme that "much can be done." He was never content simply to denounce the war and call for American withdrawal. The responsibility of the next President would be to act, not to pour out a stream of rhetoric. Kennedy's campaign was intended not only to attract votes but to attract support for positive domestic programs and a course in foreign policy that might bring an end to the war on just terms.

We can—as I have urged for two years, but as we have never done—negotiate with the National Liberation Front. We can—as we have never done—assure the Front a genuine place in the political life of South Vietnam. We can—as we are refusing to do today—begin to de-escalate the war, concentrate on protecting populated areas, and thus save American lives and slow down the destruction of the countryside. We can—as we have never done—insist that the Government of South Vietnam broaden its base, institute real reforms, and seek an honorable settlement with their fellow countrymen.[17]

While none of the other candidates in 1968, in either party, set forth so clearly what he would do about Vietnam if elected, all of them, including Kennedy, tacitly agreed to take care lest their speeches weaken the President's effort to persuade the Communists to go to the bargaining table. On the Democratic side, Vice President Humphrey was necessarily limited to defense of the administration's position, though he gave as heavy emphasis as he could to his hope for a political rather than a military settlement. McCarthy, at times, seemed to advocate immediate unilateral withdrawal, but when pressed by questioners he admitted that such a course was not practical. Otherwise, he offered few clues as to how he would conduct American policy if he were to be elected. His criticism of the strong Presidency, however, seemed to conflict with his demand for action to end the war.

Among the Republicans, Governor George Romney withdrew early, and Governor Nelson Rockefeller entered too late. The field was thus left clear for Nixon. The future President, who had previously always been numbered among the hawks, now stressed the need for a negotiated peace, but coupled his new emphasis, as did President Johnson, with strong insistence on "honorable" terms. He refused to be drawn into any statements more specific.

The debate on Vietnam died, to all practical purposes, with Kennedy. After the nominating conventions, discussion of the war was almost entirely limited to pious claims by each candidate that he could end the war more quickly than the other. Both Nixon and Humphrey favored a halt to the bombing, and President Johnson finally so ordered. Both favored a "political" settlement with an "honorable peace," and both opposed sudden, unilateral withdrawal. But neither offered an unambiguous statement as to how he would proceed if elected. Humphrey, of course, was trapped in the Johnson administration and could not effectively criticize it. Nixon, trapped by his previous belligerent attitude, could not criticize the administration effectively either. Instead he promised that he had "a plan for ending the war." What the plan might be remained wholly obscure. But it was perhaps a politically effective gambit, since Humphrey's only possible response was to ask why, if such a plan really existed, Nixon did not share it with the President.

Since there were no significant differences between the candidates, the American voters went to the polls in November unable to register their views on the war. They could not give either man a mandate, even had he asked for one, which neither did. The whole point of Robert Kennedy's campaign had been to rally majority opinion not only behind himself as a leader but behind his proposals for dealing with the war. Had he been elected the country would know what to expect—indeed, he would have been elected because the majority wanted what was expected. In the act of campaigning Kennedy was trying to educate the citizens by setting forth his own views and debating with others. But after his death the nature of the campaign was sharply altered. It was no longer a question of debating the great issues on the basis of specific proposals by the candidates, to determine what the people wished to do and whom they wished to do it. It was, instead, a contest to see who could make the least enemies, the least binding commitments, and persuade the most people that he would bring about "national unity."

Since the campaign of 1968 did not produce a national decision on Vietnam, President Nixon was forced to proceed without a mandate. The polls, of course, showed that the people were tired of the war, but no other guidance was available. When Nixon's "plan" was finally revealed, it turned out to be nothing more than training Vietnamese soldiers to take over from the Americans as rapidly as possible, thus permitting a phased withdrawal of American combat troops. This, of course, had been American policy from the beginning of intervention. What was new was to call it "Vietnamization" and to commence actually withdrawing troops. That such a program would take years to carry out was admitted. That it would do nothing to remove the causes of the insurgency was not discussed.

There is, of course, no way of knowing whether Robert Kennedy, had he lived and been elected, could have ended the war on the terms or by the means he had proposed. But if he had won, he would have had a clear mandate. And what seemed certain was that bringing the war to an end with a settlement that had a chance to last would ultimately require the kind of decisive presidential leadership for which he had campaigned, if not the specific proposals he had made.

Despite the national obsession with the Vietnam problem and his own necessary preoccupation with it, Kennedy's concern in foreign policy was by no means limited to the war. As a student of foreign affairs and as a candidate for President he gave a great deal of attention to Latin America, China, and the Middle East. As a senator he devoted much time to both travel and study as he formulated positions of his own. As his brother's closest confidant he had for three years shared in the making of foreign policy decisions and personally undertaken several special missions abroad. His quest for knowledge and for useful acquaintance with the world's leaders and peoples led him to visit most major countries and scores of minor ones. Few men have ever sought the Presidency with such thorough knowledge of the world with which a President must deal.

Every United States President must project a Latin American policy, or at the least maintain one he inherits. There is no escape from difficult decisions on problems arising in Latin America or in country-to-country relations between the United States and those nations Franklin Roosevelt hoped would be our "good neighbors." But few candidates for the Presidency have been so well prepared to conduct relations with Latin America as was Robert Kennedy, and none has ever spelled out his views more systematically. As in the case of Vietnam, there was no doubt as to what his course would be if elected.

The problem, as Kennedy analyzed it in *To Seek a Newer World*, was not simply to maintain friendly relationships with Latin American governments regardless of their character, as had so often been the American policy, but to provide massive and effective assistance for the modernization and democratization of Latin American nations. It was necessary to start with the facts of poverty, disease, and illiteracy in Latin America and to understand that in the long run the security of all the Americas, including the United States, depends on steady and rapid reduction of these evils. The alternatives were equally distasteful: either support repressive militarist regimes or allow Communists to lead successful insurgencies.

Kennedy's proposals for Latin America were much the same as his proposals for Southeast Asia, and for the same reasons. A Communist-led insurgency had already overthrown the corrupt and repressive government in Cuba, and Cuban-inspired revolutionaries were probing in various spots in Latin America for new opportunities. There had been a serious threat in Venezuela, contained only by a genuine reform program led by a democratic politician, Betancourt, and aided by the United States.

But Kennedy had seen for himself the abject poverty in which most Latin Americans lived. It would take really drastic reforms to make their lives worth living and forestall Communist-inspired civil wars.

In Venezuela [he wrote] the elections of 1963 were carried out with the greatest difficulty in the midst of terrorism; during my visit in November 1965, Caracas still resembled in many ways a city under siege by hostile forces. More significantly, these groups [Communist-led insurgent guerrillas] are often more disciplined and active than the forces of democratic reform; and all too often, they are the only group showing apparent concern for improvement in the lot of the landless peasant or the urban slum dweller. There is a village in the Andes where only one person has ever come to say that he believed in land for the peasants. That one man was a Communist, and now many of these villagers call themselves Communists, too, since they are in favor of land reform.[18]

Thus, at least in the matter of land, the problem was similar to Vietnam: the government and the landowners were either identical or inseparable. Radical reforms could not naturally arise from such age-old alliances.

Robert Kennedy had participated in earlier years in the projection of President Kennedy's Alliance for Progress. In 1968 he was urging more vigorously than ever that that stumbling plan be made to work. The Alliance, he readily admitted, had not succeeded. But its failures were understandable and avoidable. The United States was still giving aid and encouragement to precisely those governments and groups which stood in the way of the Alliance's progress. Democratic reformers were being denounced as Communist by Latin American rightwingers while the United States government seemed to concur:

. . . if we allow ourselves to become allied with those to whom the cry of "Communism" is only an excuse for the perpetuation of privilege; if we assist, with military matériel and other aid, governments that use that aid to prevent reform for their people, then we do much to ensure that reform, when it comes, will bear the Communist label.[19]

It was necessary also, Kennedy argued, to understand that military intervention in politics is almost endemic in Latin America. "Even a government of true reform is not invulnerable to armed force." Venezuela was a case in point. In 1961 President Betancourt's democratically elected reform government was "threatened on two sides: by the terrorists themselves and by the army which was close to taking over in the name of 'public order.' " Betancourt sought to meet the situation by "a crash program to combat the insurgency." The force he used was the police rather than the army. Police "trained . . . in mob and riot control, in infiltration of subversive organizations, in fast communications" managed to surmount "the immediate crisis."[20]

But the President of the United States must fully understand, Kennedy continued,

> . . . that there is much more to controlling insurgency than the training of police and controlling the military. Insurgency aims not at the conquest of territory but at the allegiance of men. In the Latin American countryside as in other threatened parts of the world, that allegiance can be won only by positive programs: by land reforms, by schools, by honest administration, by roads and clinics and labor unions and even-handed justice, and a share for all men in the decisions that shape their lives. Counterinsurgency might best be described as social reform under pressure.[21]

The moral for United States policy was that it would continue to be fatally wrong to support "any effort that disregards the base of social reform, and becomes preoccupied with gadgets and techniques and force."

> However obvious this lesson might appear, there are some within our own government, as well as some leaders of other countries, who have not recognized its teachings. For us, this failure will be costly; for others, around the world and not just in Latin America, this mistake will be their last.[22]

Kennedy had strongly opposed American intervention in the Dominican Republic in 1965. "Our determination to stop Communist revolution in the hemisphere must not be construed as opposition to popular uprisings against injustice and oppression just because the targets of such popular uprisings say they are Communist-inspired or Communist-led, or even because known Communists take part in them." The real objective of United States policy must not be to root out Communists but to root out poverty, corruption, and special privilege at the expense of the poor.

Another serious objection to a policy of intervention, like that pursued by President Johnson in the Dominican Republic, was that it was logically untenable. If thirty thousand troops were needed in a tiny island country, it took no great effort of imagination to see what would be required in a country like Brazil or Argentina. And what if incidents judged to be critical were to take place in several countries at once? The answer, Kennedy insisted, was to "realize that we cannot put down disorder everywhere in the hemisphere. If we wish to minimize the damage and danger of revolution, we must concentrate instead on programs of social improvement."

Kennedy saw Communist-led insurgency as a major problem in all underdeveloped countries, but his proposals for American policy equally emphasized the problem of diminishing military influence and expenditure. While he recognized that in some countries of Latin America, as in Asia, there were elements of reform among the military, "the day and the danger of military dictatorship are not over." The real question, therefore, was not "whether the role of the military should be diminished, but how." Primary responsibility, of course, belonged to the Latin Americans, but United States policy could and should be a potent force in "their own efforts to eliminate the military from politics."

... we should lead the way toward cutting down arms sales to Latin America. Our military representatives in each of these countries should clearly understand this to be our policy. Frequently in the past, it would appear that they have not, or if they do, they have ignored it —promoting the purchase of military equipment and the importance of the military establishment itself. Of the needlessly advanced weapons in Latin America, most were purchased—not donated by the United States; it is arms purchases, not grants, that use up valuable foreign exchange. As we are the major supplier of military arms, we should make the major effort to cut down arms sales to Latin America and other countries around the world.[23]

Kennedy understood well enough that withdrawal of the United States from the arms market would open up opportunities for other suppliers. A serious effort to diminish the military, therefore, "would require cooperation with our European allies." There was no easy way to do it, of course, but "cooperation comes out of leadership, which we must be willing to exercise."

On the primary campaign trails there were few of the opportunities to talk about Latin American policy that there would have been in the presidential contest with the Republican candidate. But Kennedy often tied the problem of insurgency in Latin America into his talks on Vietnam. At the University of Indiana, for example, he spoke of the "nations of Latin America which are Western but not yet modern." They would, he said, "be plagued by instability for decades to come."

... we should offer to their effort such assistance as we can, or what will be effective.

But we cannot continue as we often have done in the past to automatically identify the United States with the preservation of a particular internal order within those countries or confuse our own national interests with the rule of a particular faction within them. Of course, those in power in these countries will often seek to preserve their position by requesting our help.

In the face of such requests, he continued, "we must make calm and discriminating judgments as to which governments can and should be helped." He proposed two criteria for making such judgments: that governments "are moving effectively to defend themselves and meet the needs of their people," and that "we should give no more assistance to a government against any internal threat than that government is capable of using itself, through its agencies and instruments."[24] Thus American intervention would be ruled out, and military approaches to internal crises would be diminished so far as possible.

In the campaign between Nixon and Humphrey little was said about Latin America. Again, the Vice President was part of the administration which had intervened in the Dominican Republic and had failed to put serious pressure on Latin American governments to move ahead with Alliance for Progress agreements on economic and political reforms. Nixon, who had been spat upon in Latin America when, as Vice President, he had made a "good will" tour, avoided any mention of the armament problem. His infrequent comments were confined chiefly to rhetoric about the dangers of communism and the need for friendly relations with our Latin neighbors. As candidate and as President, Nixon did upon occasion speak of the "new approaches" that "new leadership" would bring. But after Governor Nelson Rockefeller's trying experiences on his tour of Latin America in 1969, the Nixon administration proposed little more than a reform of tariff rates and import quotas to encourage trade.

The Rockefeller Report itself provided heavy documentation of the poverty and misery throughout most of Latin America. But while it warned against the influence of American "special interests" it advocated more rather than less military assistance, including providing heavy weapons, jet aircraft, and even warships to the larger nations.[25] Nothing was said in the report or by President Nixon about encouraging the peaceful revolution Kennedy had proposed, nor was any alternative suggested for dealing with the inescapable problems he had believed an American President must tackle.

Before and during the campaign of 1968 Robert Kennedy often took sharply defined positions on other major problems of foreign policy. In a remarkable address at a University of Chicago symposium, for example, he advocated drastic revision of United States policy toward China, including progress toward recognition:

> Policy demands finally a conscious and open recognition that we live in the same world and move in the same continent with China—with its dangers and possibilities, strengths and terrible frustrations. Only when we accept this reality can we work toward our central task: to bring about Chinese acceptance of the fact that it too must live with us and the other nations of the world.[26]

In many campaign speeches he talked of the insurgency threat in Thailand, of the struggles going on in Indonesia and elsewhere in Southeast Asia, and of the need to redirect the Atlantic alliance toward reconstruction and development in Africa and Asia. Always he pledged to direct American policy toward peaceful, nonmilitary solutions to fundamental problems. Candidate Nixon, for his part, said little about China and little about Southeast Asia. But as President he approached China in terms like those Kennedy had advocated. And his Guam statement of a "Nixon Doctrine," again, suggested Kennedy's urgent call for de-emphasizing military solutions to political, social, and economic problems in the developing nations.

There is one issue on which all presidential candidates have agreed for twenty years—Israel. But there are ways of pledging continuing American support for the state of Israel which are *pro forma*, and ways which are tough and specific. While McCarthy, Humphrey, and Nixon all asserted the necessity of maintaining Israel's integrity, and McCarthy, in answer to questions, favored shipments of jet fighters to Israel, Kennedy, characteristically, was tougher and more specific. He used the same language in many campaign speeches. For example, at Portland, Oregon toward the end of his losing campaign in that state, he contrasted Israel with Vietnam to show why he favored all-out support for the one but not for the other.

[Israel] is the very opposite of Vietnam. Israel's government is democratic, effective, free of corruption; its people are united in its support. Our commitment to Israel reflects the fact that the Israelis—as they made so courageously clear during the June war—will not ask us to do their job for them. To help Israel defend her security, as a matter of morality and as a matter of practicality, is in our most basic national interest. That commitment—that twenty-year-old promise to assure Israel's security must be kept.[27]

He went on to discuss the problem of the arms race. The fact was that the Arabs were receiving "massive arms aid" from the Soviet Union. The Soviet Union was sending impressive naval strength into the Mediterranean and providing advisers to Arab armies.

As long as this imbalance continues, those who seek Israel's destruction will be encouraged to plan a fourth round of war. In my judgement, the United States cannot permit this kind of imbalance. We must keep Israel secure against outside agression—with arms, if necessary. *That requires now the selling to Israel of the fifty Phantom jets she has so long been promised. There should be no further delay. This commitment must be fulfilled now.* We all desire an end to the arms race. But it cannot be unilateral—for such a course promises only more aggression and threat of yet another bloody conflict.[28]

Again it is not possible to say whether Kennedy's leadership in pressing such a policy in the Middle East would have been effective in stabilizing that most tortured area of hate and war. What is certain is that the voters would have known what they were going to get had he been elected, whereas in the aftermath of his death the election of 1968 gave no guidance to the winner beyond the broad generalization that Israel should be permitted to exist. When President Nixon seemed to cultivate the Arabs in the early years of his administration there were uncomfortable reminders of the policy John Foster Dulles had conducted in the Eisenhower years, a policy that collapsed in the Suez War of 1956. The Israelis, rightly or wrongly, again felt let down by their American friends, and despite the firming up of American support for Israel and the United Nations peace effort, no end to the war was in sight.

There was never any doubt in the spring of 1968 that Robert Kennedy meant what he said. At least one young man resolved for this very reason that Kennedy should not become President. Whatever other insane motives may have led Sirhan Sirhan to murder Kennedy, he left no doubt that he intended to help the Arab cause by eliminating the strongest proponent of Israel among the presidential candidates. He may also have eliminated the issue from the election.

THREE

The Cities: Poverty, Race, and Crime

The national preoccupation with the Vietnam war at the outset of the 1968 presidential campaign at times almost smothered other issues or, in some cases, absorbed them. It was commonplace, for example, to blame the outbreaks of riot and other violence in the cities on the war—money that would have alleviated human suffering was wasted on the war; disillusioned blacks were rebelling against their exploitation as cannon fodder; black rebels called themselves guerrillas in the vanguard of a coming American revolution inspired by Che Guevara, Ho Chi Minh, and Mao Tse-tung. This simplistic approach to endemic problems developing into permanent crises contained perhaps some kernels of truth. But, whatever uses it may have had as political propaganda, it was at the best a futile exercise in urban reform. The problems were much older than the war and would persist long after the war was over.

All of the presidential candidates, of course, knew this well enough. But Richard Nixon had never displayed any serious grasp of either the problem of poverty or the crisis in race relations. He had served eight years under President Eisenhower in an administration which had avoided, so far as it could, taking any of the potentially divisive measures needed to arrest urban decay and lead the country toward equality among the races. Nixon's opposition to crime was sufficiently forthright to gladden the hearts of those distressed and confused people whose resentment of unsafe streets was being heard in ever more strident tones. But he said little about the causes of violence.

Hubert Humphrey, in contrast, had amply displayed his concern for many years. His name was identified with not a few of the measures by which government was trying to cope with problems that seemed to become less rather than more manageable with the years. But Humphrey's approach was no longer marked by innovation. His humanitarianism called, or so it seemed, for little more than heavier federal spending, not radical reform. Eugene McCarthy, too, seemed to offer only a prospect of trying to narrow the poverty gap by a greater flow of federal dollars and greater reliance on already floundering local governments. Robert Kennedy, for his part, not only went well beyond his rivals in the new approaches he suggested, but left no doubt that he saw the problems of the cities as the paramount issue before the country, war or no war.

Kennedy had been almost overwhelmed by the dimensions of poverty and decay and crime that he had found in the cities of New York State during his 1964 campaign for the Senate. Thereafter he had devoted more time and energy to the search for policies and programs for effective reform and to active experimentation than to any other matter. He had commissioned staff studies, enlisted the advice of specialists in the universities, collaborated on new legislation with such colleagues as Senator Jacob Javits, and familiarized himself personally with the leaders of civic organizations working on urban reform. In a ceaseless effort to understand the feelings of the dispossessed and the alienated, he cultivated and extended his acquaintance with black leaders and their ghetto followers, not only in New York but throughout the country. He hoped and believed that he could persuade them that the American system, if pushed hard and effectively directed, would provide resolutions of their problems with a better kind of life for all as a consequence.

While he spoke out on behalf of the civil rights demonstrations and marches in the South, Kennedy insisted from the outset of his career in the Senate and as a national Democratic leader that the plight of black Americans was not regional but national and not to be separated from the general misery of the poor in the city ghettoes.

. . . the many brutalities of the North [he said in 1965] receive no such attention [as in the South]. I have been in tenements in Harlem in the past several weeks where the smell of rats was so strong that it was difficult to stay there for five minutes, and where children slept with lights turned on their feet to discourage attacks.

In central Harlem, over 50 percent of all housing units are seriously deteriorating or dilapidated, as opposed to about 10 percent of housing units in this condition occupied by whites. Thousands do not flock to Harlem to protest these conditions—much less to change them.[1]

One is reminded of Theodore Roosevelt in the 1890s reluctantly following Jacob A. Riis into the New York garment district to learn for himself what sweatshops were like. Roosevelt was converted to progressivism by the experience. Robert Kennedy was already bent on reform in 1964, but his experience in New York ghettoes turned thoughtful concern into passionate commitment.

It was this commitment, more than any program, which gave Kennedy's campaign for President its tone and spirit of urgency. And it was the urgency, perhaps, which won and held his devoted following among the poor, especially the black poor. But he was asking the voters for a good deal more than trust. He made extensive specific proposals, in part based on positions he had already taken and on experiments in urban rehabilitation he had inspired. By 1968 "the word" had long been "out" that Kennedy was not just a talker.

He had started from the premise that the idea of breaking up the ghettoes by dispersal of the blacks and other minorities into the suburbs or "new towns," however theoretically desirable, was little more than rhetoric when the dimensions of the problem were squarely faced. And there was danger also that the goal of dispersal, precisely because it was largely rhetorical, might serve to obviate really effective action—especially federal initiative and funding—to eliminate ghetto poverty and squalor.

How immense the problem was, in realistic terms, Kennedy set forth in testimony before a committee of his fellow senators in 1966:

Segregation is becoming the governing rule: Washington is only the most prominent example of a city which has become overwhelmingly Negro as whites move to the suburbs; many other cities are moving along the same road—for example, Chicago, which if present trends continue will be over 50 percent Negro by 1975. The ghettoes of Harlem and Southside and Watts are cities in themselves, areas of as much as 350,000 people.

With segregation went "endemic" poverty and unemployment: ". . . from one-third to one-half of the families in these areas live in poverty; in some male unemployment may be as high as 40 percent; unemployment of Negro youths nationally is over 25 percent." And with poverty went dependency on welfare: ". . . one fourth of the children in these ghettoes, as in Harlem, may receive Federal Aid to Dependent Children; in New York City, ADC alone costs over $20 million a month; in our five largest cities, the ADC bill is over $500 million a year."

Housing, Kennedy continued, was overcrowded, unhealthy, and dilapidated with "43 percent of urban Negro housing substandard." But worst of all was the wretched state of health care.

. . . ten thousand children may be injured or infected by rat bites every year. . . . infant mortality in the ghettoes is more than twice the rate outside; mental retardation caused by inadequate prenatal care is more than seven times the white rate; one-half of all babies born in Manhattan last year will have had no prenatal care at all; deaths from diseases like tuberculosis, influenza, and pneumonia are two to three times as common as elsewhere.[2]

Under such conditions, Kennedy was persuaded, it simply would not do to talk smugly about the progress black Americans had made and were still making in the political field. The empathy he more and more felt for the ghetto blacks and successfully communicated to them was often expressed in poignant words. The Labor Department, he told an audience honoring Paul Douglas in 1967, "has explained that the youth of the slums 'just don't have the connections.' "

There are, of course, connections they can make. For a few blocks away, or on a television set, the young man can watch the multiplying marvels of white America: new cars and new homes, air conditioners and outdoor barbecues. Every day television commercials tell him that life is impossible without the latest products of our consumer society. But he cannot buy them. He is told that the Negro is making progress. But what does that mean to him?

What it meant, as Kennedy saw it, was simply that the young black American, unable to experience the progress of the whites, could not be expected to feel grateful or to stay quietly in his place without protest:

... nor should we seriously expect him to feel grateful because he is no longer a slave, or because he can vote or eat at some lunch counters. For he compares his condition not with the past, but with the life of other Americans. ... Now, as ever, it is when submission gives way to expectation, when despair is touched with the awareness of possibility, that the forces of human desire and the passion for justice are unloosed.[3]

More even than discrimination, Kennedy came to feel, as he learned to appreciate the condition of man in the ghetto, it was unemployment which underlay the misery of both young and old, especially as it sapped the sense of confidence and dignity of young men. In Harlem and in Bedford-Stuyvesant he found that unemployment averaged 10 percent or more, as against a national average at that time of less than 4 percent. But "unemployment of young Negroes, seeking to establish their identity and their manhood, is estimated at an even greater percent."[4]

For a time Kennedy simply supported as vigorously as he could the measures of the Office of Economic Opportunity and the Labor Department to train or retrain unemployed blacks and others in the slums to fit them for jobs. The assumption behind these programs, sound enough in itself, was that lack of education, often coupled with habituation to jobs swept away by technological changes, was the evil most needing to be remedied. But experience in Harlem and Bedford-Stuyvesant showed that the results were wholly unsatisfactory. Sometimes, indeed, job training made a situation worse. The deeper problem, as Kennedy discovered, was that there were no jobs to be filled. Businesses had simply left or were leaving the slums, and leaving the labor force behind.

. . . no government program now operating gives any substantial promise of meeting the problem of Negro unemployment in the ghetto. The Manpower Development and Training Act, the Vocational Education Act . . .—these and similar efforts have been going on for five years. Yet in these same five years, while family income nationwide was increasing 14 percent, and family income of Negroes nationwide was increasing 24 percent, family income in Watts *dropped* 8 percent.

Under such circumstances "high school seniors who see last year's graduates standing on street corners—or working part-time at menial jobs—are not likely to be impressed with the value of last year's schooling."[5]

The unanswerable logic of the crisis in the cities, he concluded, was that "it is not enough, in this technological society, to hire qualified Negroes, nor even to raise the number that are qualified; we must create new jobs for all that can work, regardless of their level of skill."[6]

Not the least of the evils of poverty and unemployment in the ghettoes of the cities, of course, is the rapidly growing incidence of violence and crime. From his days on the McClellan Committee investigating crime in labor unions, through his years of responsibility for law enforcement Robert Kennedy had been thoroughly familiar with the alarming statistics. As Attorney General, he had learned to gauge the impact of crime on American society. But it was direct experience again, in New York City slums as well as in the ghettoes of other cities after his election to the Senate, that brought home to him the terrible interrelatedness of violence, crime, and the poverty and alienation of Americans in the ghetto from other Americans. Often enough, he found, "there is no point in telling Negroes to obey the law, because to many Negroes the law is the enemy."[7]

But to understand was not to condone. In a 1966 speech to the University of California at Berkeley, where a cult of violence had already gained an alarming number of adherents, Kennedy stressed the pervasive evils of lawlessness and violence:

We must oppose violence not because of what violence does to the possibility of cooperation between whites and blacks; not just because it hampers the passage of civil rights bills, or poverty legislation, or open-occupancy laws.

The central disease of violence is what it does to all of us—to those who engage in it as much as to those who are its victims.

Granted that "cruelty and wanton violence may temporarily relieve a feeling of frustration, a sense of impotence"— surely the chief cause of ghetto riots—"but the damage to those who perpetrate it," he said, is "the negation of reason and the antithesis of humanity, and they are the besetting sins of the twentieth century. Surely the world has seen enough, in the last forty years, of violence and hatred."[8]

Kennedy spoke in the same way, sometimes even more pointedly, to black audiences. While "we have a long way to go before the law means the same thing to Negroes as it does to us" was a statement often reiterated in his speeches to all kinds of groups, he did not hesitate to tell black leaders that theirs was "a heavy responsibility. . . . it is you— leaders of the Negro American Community—who know what must be done better than white Americans can ever know—you must take the lead; you who must take the first steps, using what is available, and showing what is needed but not available."[9]

And ghetto violence was not the kind of first step to take. The "violent youth of the ghetto," Kennedy conceded, was "not simply protesting his condition, but trying to assert his worth and dignity as a human being." But violence is "destructive and self-defeating." The militant leaders, like Rap Brown, who shouted slogans of revolution and threatened to "burn America down," were not revolutionaries. They were anarchists. The end, Kennedy said, "is not a better life for Negroes, but a devastated America."[10]

In all his discussion of crime after 1964, Kennedy sought to emphasize the unequal treatment of the law as between the affluent and the poor, black or white. He had been a crime fighter throughout his public career—sometimes so persistent and tough that liberals had accused him of being overzealous. But to fight crime, he insisted, must not be an end in itself. Equal justice under law was the higher objective. His favorite example was the problem of bail. "Punishment," he told a governors' conference in 1965, "is imposed in thousands of cases simply because the defendant is ·poor."

In most jurisdictions, from one-third to one-half or more of those accused of crime will be acquitted, or have their charges dismissed. Many more will have their sentences suspended, or be allowed to pay a fine. In fact, less than 10 percent of those arrested in New York City can expect to be sentenced to prison terms. But for thousands of these, . . . poverty will rule that the mere act of arrest will result in imprisonment—and the loss of job, self-respect, separation from family, and possible ruin. This is not the law of reason.[11]

Another persistent problem Kennedy sought to resolve was recidivism, the return to criminal life by a released convict. Again, his approach to the problem was to seek the cause and find means to correct it. "We must educate and vocationally train those who are in prison." But training for rehabilitation, long under way in many prisons, was not enough, for the same reason that the manpower retraining program was not enough. "We must be prepared to supply guidance and help find employment for those who are released from incarceration facilities."[12] No matter how glowing the statistics of economic growth in the United States, no matter how many were employed or how few were unemployed, Kennedy always came back to the fact that there were millions of poor people and thousands of criminals all over the country whose rebellious state of mind was largely owing to the lack of a decent job with a decent income.

What was needed was a real revolution in the cities. The only way to bring about controlled and creative change was "to bring these problems into the political process—to make them the subject of public action." And the leadership of white liberals could not be enough; "more leadership will have to come from Negroes themselves." Kennedy's experimental response to his own challenge was the Bedford-Stuyvesant Project.

The Bedford-Stuyvesant Project is now so well known throughout the country and elsewhere in the world that there is no need to describe it in detail here. What is important is that experience in an ambitious practical effort to treat poverty, crime, racism, and urban decay as different aspects of one inclusive problem lay behind Robert Kennedy's proposals to the nation as a candidate for President in 1968.

In a sense the project had its beginnings in an amendment to the Economic Opportunity Act of 1966 offered by Kennedy and his New York Republican colleague Jacob Javits. Under that amendment Congress authorized an initial sum of $26 million to be spent in experimental programs of urban rehabilitation. Known as the "Special Impact Program," the law provided for assistance to community development corporations and to private businesses which would plan the regeneration of ghetto areas and create employment opportunities. Emphasis was on economic development, but funds were also made available to stimulate housing, health, education, and vocational training. Making use of this law, Kennedy took the leadership in forming two public corporations to regenerate the Bedford-Stuyvesant area of Brooklyn with its four hundred thousand mostly black residents living near or below the poverty line.

On December 9, 1966 Kennedy announced the formation of a Community Development Corporation, composed of residents of Bedford-Stuyvesant, to plan all phases of a comprehensive program—housing, education, health, recreation, and above all, new industries to provide stable employment. At the same time, he announced that another corporation, composed mainly of eminent leaders in industry and banking, had been formed to assist the project with professional advice, and by raising money from foundations and attracting business into the area.

Bedford-Stuyvesant was an ambitious project. Some writers called it Robert Kennedy's "private war on poverty." But what is important here is simply that the project greatly enriched Kennedy's practical experience in leadership and organization, and demonstrated both to himself and to the country the kind of attack on social problems he would lead as President.

In *To Seek a Newer World*, Kennedy gathered material from several of his earlier statements, updated important statistics, and elaborated a number of his concerns about the condition of the ghetto blacks in a substantial chapter called "Race and the City: The Slums and Community." This chapter, in turn, provided much of the material for campaign speeches in the spring of 1968. The central theme of the essay, as of his campaign itself, was the need for decent jobs to enable the ghetto poor—black, Puerto Rican, Mexican-American, or white—to realize dignity as human beings and acquire hope for a satisfying life.

Above all, Kennedy sought to see the problem as young slum dwellers were seeing it. "Through the eyes of the white majority," he wrote, "of a man of decent impulse and moral purpose, the Negro world is one of steady and continuous progress."[13] With the ending of legal discrimination, the emergence of blacks in eminent public positions, and the reform programs enacted by Congress, the white American found himself frankly baffled by the riots, the threats of greater violence, and the nearly universal dissatisfaction of the Negroes. Many bitterly rejected the claims of the blacks, many were frightened. "But if we look through the eyes of the young slum dweller—the Negro, the Puerto-Rican, the Mexican-American—there is a different view." From *his* perspective, Kennedy wrote, "the world is a hopeless place indeed." If one seriously tried to discover the reasons, they were not hard to find:

The chances are that he was born into a family without a father—often as a result of welfare laws that require a broken home as a condition of help. His chance of dying in the first year of life is twice that of children born outside the ghetto; and because his mother rarely saw a doctor, his chances of being mentally retarded are seven times the community average.

But the young person through whose eyes we are now looking has, at least, survived. What of his growing years?

He may spend his childhood crowded with adults into one or two rooms, without adequate plumbing or heat, with rats his companions of the night. He goes to a school which teaches little that can help him in an alien world. His chances of graduating from high school are three out of ten; and if he does graduate, there is only a fifty-fifty chance that he will have even the equivalent of an eighth-grade education.

Kennedy punctuated this dismaying account with the words of "a young college graduate who taught in a slum school: 'The books are junk, the paint peels, the cellar stinks, the teachers call you nigger, the window falls on your head.' "

After whatever schooling he gets, the slum-dweller is stuck in a place where "stores charge inflated prices for shoddy goods; forty-three percent of . . . housing is substandard and overcrowded." College education is for most a simple impossibility. In a "typical recent year," Kennedy pointed out, only thirty-seven out of more than a quarter of a million Puerto Rican children in New York were in college.

Underlying all the misery and hopelessness, in Kennedy's view, was the lack of decent jobs. "Worst of all, the people of the ghetto and the barrio live today with an unemployment rate worse than the rest of the nation knew during the depth of the Great Depression." And it is difficult even to know how many are unemployed in the decayed cities of today:

The measure of the crisis of joblessness is not to be found in traditional unemployment figures, although these tell of crisis enough. The official statistics tell us that unemployment in the ghettoes of poverty —among Negroes in Hough, Mexican-Americans in East Los Angeles, Appalachian whites in Chicago, Puerto-Ricans in East Harlem, Indians on reservations—is over three times the national rate. But these figures do not count the full extent of the problem, because the whole apparatus of government cannot even find from one-fifth to one-third of the adult men of the ghetto.

Such are the facts of life for the young slum-dweller.

How overwhelming must be the frustration of this young man— this young American—who, desperately wanting to believe and half-believing, finds himself locked in slums, his education second-rate, unable to get a job [one-fourth of those who have jobs earn less than sixty dollars a week, the poverty line] confronted by the open prejudice and subtle hostilities of a white world, and seemingly powerless to change his condition or shape his future.

It is easy, and proper, to tell him to work his way up "as other minorities have done." But he cannot do so if he cannot get a job. "The jobs have fled to the suburbs, or been replaced by machines, or have moved beyond the reach of those with limited education and skills." Thus the young American of the slum "feels denied membership in that American society to which by birth and natural allegiance he belongs." It was in the frustration and the bitterness of this alienation that Kennedy found the source of the violence, the crime, even the drug addiction that poison the ghettoes and with them the whole of American life.

What was novel about Kennedy's treatment of the inter-related problems of race, crime, and poverty in the cities was not just detailing of the facts, though no other presidential candidate ever took such pains to learn and to explain them, but the determination with which he sought to confront and overcome them. Rejecting expanded welfare programs as merely palliative, and denying the short-run practicability of dispersal of ghetto populations, he pinned his hope for the future on programs to create jobs, both in the work of rebuilding slums and in permanent new industries and services in the regenerated areas.

The process of community development must begin on an economic base: a foundation of individual and community self-support, at last escaping from degrading and imprisoning dependency. . . .

To have a maximum impact on the problems of the poor, the new enterprises must be established, the new jobs must be created, in the ghetto itself.

Such jobs, Kennedy believed, would have "an important multiplier effect" in creating other jobs. He cited experience under the Area Redevelopment Act to show that for every three jobs created in a new industrial facility, from two to three additional jobs arise in related activities. So it would be in the ghettoes. At the time he wrote *To Seek a Newer World* the Bedford-Stuyvesant Project was too recently begun to provide conclusive evidence, but Kennedy described the experiment and reported that already there were hopeful signs that it would succeed.

The success of community development in Bedford-Stuyvesant or elsewhere would depend heavily on private enterprise.

Government at all levels—Federal, state and local—will have to play key roles in any such program. But total reliance on government would be a mistake. It would not only be astronomically costly to the taxpayer; more important, it would make the program, the people of the ghetto, totally dependent on politics—on year-to-year appropriations, and the favor of others. Rather the projects must be self-sustaining, generate income for the community, and have a multiplier effect in improving its economic health.

Here was what Richard Nixon was to call "black capitalism." But in Kennedy's view, the black businessmen could at first provide only a small part of the economic growth. Outside industry must provide the great initial push, as in Bedford-Stuyvesant. And government's contribution would be both a generating and a sustaining factor for years to come.

To encourage private development Kennedy introduced bills to give tax incentives to industries willing to locate plants in the reviving city slums and to make low-interest loans available to construction firms that would build low-rent housing in the same areas.

In sum, Kennedy's proposals and practical experiments called for a great new effort of cooperation among government, business, and the people of the ghettoes:

Everything that is done must be in direct response to the needs and wishes of the people themselves. To do this, it will be necessary to create new community institutions that local residents control, and through which they can express their wishes. . . .
. . . community corporations would ensure that what is done to create jobs and build homes builds the community as well . . . not just the physical development of the community, but the development of its educational system, its health services—in short, all the services its residents need.

Kennedy offered numerous suggestions for theaters, parks, playgrounds, clubhouses and other community facilities which could be built, with profit to the community, by community corporations. But it is enough for the purpose here to see that by 1968 he had laid a solid foundation for a campaign for the Presidency and for an administration directed to radical reform. On the most urgent problems of the country, more pressing and foreboding even than the Vietnam war, he knew what he wished to say, what proposals he would make, what he thought should be done and how—if he were elected President, he would seek to do it.

Campaigning for proposals to regenerate the cities, reconcile hostile groups, and bring home the alienated was of a different order of politics from attacking President Johnson's Vietnam policy. The war was already widely unpopular and presented a rather simple issue: the problem was to persuade greater numbers to join the already great numbers who opposed the war on principle or were simply tired of it. Eugene McCarthy had shown how it could be done by his campaign in New Hampshire. And Kennedy was himself the national leader of opposition to the war. But the bitter divisions of people over race, crime, and poverty would not yield to strokes of wit or to expressions of moral fervor. Kennedy's quarrel with Lyndon Johnson was not so much that he had failed to attack critical social problems as that his Great Society had been subordinated to the war to such an extent as almost to disappear. Because Kennedy believed that the crisis today could only be overcome by radical measures which in their nature could not be unanimously approved, his own proposals were inherently divisive. Thus, the political problem he faced was to explain to everyone who would listen and to persuade as many as possible that the kind of partisan presidential leadership he offered was both necessary and practical.

It would be easy to go into Harlem or Watts or Hough and display once more his undoubted sympathy for the poor, especially, of course, the blacks. It would be easy to damn discrimination before groups of liberals and intellectuals. It would be easy to recite to businessmen and suburban women's clubs his record as a crime fighter. He could bemoan the fouling of the environment before any audience. But to win the Presidency with a mandate to act it was necessary to tell every audience that poverty and crime could not in the long run be treated separately, and that racial prejudice was a poison wherever it occurred. Kennedy was wholly confident that a President would be ineffective on any other terms.

Some political opponents charged Kennedy with talking tough against crime before blue-collar and white-collar audiences, while soft-talking his crowds in the ghettoes. The record was quite otherwise, as his listeners well knew. In Indiana, for example, where his critics charged him with catering to a traditional conservatism, he had this to say on April 10 before a Scottish Rite banquet:

... many Negroes—especially among the young—are losing faith in the good will and purpose of the nation and its institutions. Frustrated hope and loss of faith breed desperation. And desperate men take to the streets. I say this not to condone such violence, but merely to state a fact—a fact which can now be seen in the streets on every television screen. We may not like this fact, but we ignore it at our peril. . . . If we allow hostility or fear to blind ourselves to this reality it will be destructive to the health of this country . . . . There is no sure way to suppress men filled with anger who feel they have nothing to lose.[14]

This was hardly "papering over the issues"—which he had promised not to do at the outset of his campaign.

He knew the streets whereof he spoke. Martin Luther King had been murdered less than a week earlier (April 4, 1968). The cities were kindled and some were in flames. Kennedy walked in the ghettoes of Washington, seeking to reassure his black friends and help them to persuade their outraged fellows that violence only dishonored the memory of King and set back the movement he had led. In the streets of Gary and Hammond and South Bend he denounced violence and lawlessness at the same time that he pledged to work for the end of ghetto poverty and deprivation. He refused to separate cause and effect. Later in the month he spelled out his position before a Democratic luncheon—mostly a white audience—again in Indianapolis:

We can never even think about an end to crime or a "victory" in the war on crime or even reversing the current crime trend, unless we reach into the well springs of deprivation and frustration, of denial and anger in which the germs of crime breed; unless we address ourselves to the problems of poverty and ignorance and disease and unemployment which still mar the face of our country. In the last analysis, that is the real antidote to crime—the real protection for our lives and our homes, our children and our future. This is the effort we began 200 years ago—the struggle for equal opportunity in freedom.[15]

These words were the end, not the beginning, of a speech on crime and how to prevent it; this was what Kennedy wished his listeners to understand and to remember.

He had been campaigning in Indiana on April 4 when the news of Martin Luther King's murder reached him. King had become his friend, not easily or quickly, but finally and firmly. Years before, when he was Attorney General, Kennedy had more than one difficult meeting with King on the disobedience movement that King was leading in the South. As the nation's responsible law enforcement officer, he had to protect as best he could both white and black, and, to many blacks, at least some agents of the Justice Department appeared to be prejudiced or even bigoted. But confrontations between the Attorney General and the black leaders were gradually transformed into conversations as each learned to respect and to trust the other. Between King and Kennedy cooperation in the national interest replaced hostility and eventually became a warm and personal friendship.

At Indianapolis on April 4, 1968, it would have been easy for Kennedy, shocked and overwrought by the news, to go among the black people simply to grieve with them as a sympathetic friend. But his instinct for leadership led him to convert the occasion into a moving, extemporaneous, plea for reconciliation: "In this difficult day, in this difficult time for the United States, it is perhaps well to ask what kind of a nation we are and what direction we want to move in." "For those of you who are black," he said—and he was addressing a street-corner crowd mainly of blacks—"considering the evidence there evidently is that there were white people who were responsible—you can be filled with bitterness, with hatred, and a desire for revenge." That would mean "great polarization—black people against black, white people against white, filled with hatred toward one another." And this would be entirely understandable, especially to a Kennedy.

For those of you who are black and are tempted to be filled with hatred and distrust at the injustice of such an act, against all white people, I can only say that I feel in my own heart the same kind of feeling. I had a member of my family killed, but he was killed by a white man. But we have to make an effort in the United States, we have to make an effort to understand, to go beyond these rather difficult times.

For a long time after that many black people spoke of King's murder as a death in the family.

But beyond the grief and the bitterness, Kennedy wished them to catch his vision of a reunited country and, as a candidate for President, to lead them toward its realization:

What we need in the United States is not division; what we need in the United States is not hatred; what we need in the United States is not violence or lawlessness, but love and wisdom, and compassion toward one another, and a feeling of justice toward those who still suffer within our country, whether they be white or they be black.

At the end he asked them to say a prayer, "to say a prayer for the family of Martin Luther King, that's true, but more importantly to say a prayer for our own country, which all of us love—a prayer for understanding and that compassion of which I spoke."

But the vast majority of white people and the vast majority of black people in this country want to live together, want to improve the quality of our life, and want justice for all human beings who abide in our land.

Let us dedicate ourselves to what the Greeks wrote so many years ago: to tame the savageness of man and to make gentle the life of this world.

Let us dedicate ourselves to that, and say a prayer for our country and for our people.[16]

The next day, before a predominantly white audience in Denver, Kennedy spoke bluntly of the meaning of King's life:

We must be honest with ourselves and realize that Martin Luther King, while a hero to his race and respected by all of us, was considered a dangerous man by many white Americans. He advocated change they did not want in ways they did not like. He lighted corners of our country they prefer to keep in darkness. He and the peaceful movement he represented threatened to upset three hundred years in this country in which Negroes and Mexican-Americans and Indian-Americans have been second-class citizens.

He drew the moral frankly, despite its evident unpopularity in some quarters of Denver and elsewhere:

The difficult road, but the only one, is for white America to recognize the fundamental injustice of minority life in the United States. The difficult task, but the necessary one, is a major and immediate effort to uproot the conditions which keep these men and women from fully participating in the American system. After the riots last year the Commission headed by the Governor of Illinois analyzed the problem and made all the recommendations necessary. The plans are there, the resources are there. All we lack is the will—the will to see that the greatest threat is not change but our continued resistance to it.

Scarcely two months later, when he was himself assassinated, the Black Panther paper carried a hideous cartoon showing Kennedy lying in a pool of blood with the head of a pig. But the two close friends who caught and held Kennedy's assassin in Los Angeles until the police could take him into custody were blacks. And in the days following, all across the country and in New York City and along the railroad to Washington, the grieving crowds were mingled, not divided by color.

There were, or course, unusual, even unique, circumstances in the relations between Robert Kennedy and the black, and other, minorities. But what was essential in his campaign for President and what is indispensable in the Presidency itself is precisely the compassion and the trust he sought to invoke. For it was compassion, as Kennedy felt it, which led him to see and drove him to make others see that compassion is in itself only the beginning:

Most people, of both races, do not wish violence and agree that we must do everything we can to protect the life and property of our people. Of course, this is so. Yet while the necessary troops and police patrol our streets, we must also be aware that punishment is not prevention nor is an armed camp a place of peace. Our nation today is beset by apprehension and fears, anger and even hatred. It is easy to understand the springs of such passion: even as we know the highest traditions of this country forbid them. But today's difficulties cannot be answered simply by appeals to brotherhood or compassion. The issue is not whether white Americans will help black Americans, but whether we help ensure the well-being of every citizen.

Again he was speaking to a white audience in Indiana, trying to win a Democratic primary election in the midst of political crosscurrents running like riptides. The old coalition, formed under Franklin Roosevelt in the 1930s, seemed to be breaking up. To get enough votes to win it was necessary to hold large numbers of trade union workers once militant but now anxious for the security of their families and their homes, to reassure blacks always mostly Democratic but now alienated by continuing poverty and discrimination, to persuade rural people that the crime and violence of the cities could not simply be suppressed by force, and at the same time to convince business and professional people of the affluent middle class that radical measures to meet frightening problems would cost far less in the long run than the disastrous combination of repression and neglect. The issue, Kennedy told all his audiences in every corner of the state, "is not whether white and black will love one another—but whether they will love America. It is not whether we will enforce the laws of the nation—but whether there is to be one nation."[17]

In this spirit and with this sense of urgency Kennedy proposed the policies and programs he would undertake if he became President. "The most immediate need," he told a rally at Gary, "is for a national impact project: to put men to work, to restore possibility to the young and to give the resident of the ghetto some sense that the nation is committed to the fulfillment of his hopes."[18] He would begin with money already on hand or in sight, with drastic reordering of national priorities if necessary. "We can slow down the race to the moon, if it means the salvation of our nation here on earth. We can postpone work on the supersonic transport, if it means that we can safely sit still in our cities." Research and development could be redirected "to search for purpose and human dignity within our own communities." Above all, de-escalating the war in Vietnam should produce substantial funds for investment in the reconstruction of the nation. "We must now commit ourselves to the proposition that as funds begin to be released from Vietnam, they will come home to the service of our domestic peace."

The way to invest the funds thus shaken loose, Kennedy proposed, was in the creation of jobs:

There is work here [in the cities] for all—in the service of the most urgent public needs of the nation; work that will benefit white and black, fortunate and deprived alike. Throughout our cities there are millions of deteriorated and dilapidated housing units. City hospitals and school classrooms are overcrowded and outdated everywhere; tens of thousands of young men and women cannot attend college simply because there is no room. In fact, the inventory is almost infinite—parks and playgrounds to be built, public facilities to be renovated, new transportation networks to be established, rivers and beaches to be cleansed of filth and again made fit for human use.

With so much to be done, he said, "let us stop thinking of the poor—the dropouts, the unemployed, those on welfare, and those who work for poverty wages—let us stop thinking of them as liabilities. Let us see them for what they are: valuable resources. . . ."[19]

Kennedy spelled out a seven-point program of action: 1) The jobs as far as possible should be for the residents of the ghettoes—as "the best antidote to the debilitating and degrading welfare system"; 2) Government training programs should concentrate on the new jobs—"for too long government programs have trained men for jobs that do not exist—and thus have fed the very frustration they were designed to cure"; 3) The private sector with its "talent and the energy to undertake this awesome task" should be encouraged to do so by tax credits, tax deductions, and depreciation benefits. Businesses owned by the poor themselves should be financed by "a program of development loans—which I shall shortly introduce in the Senate"; 4) "The educational system should be directly integrated with this reconstruction effort." Dropouts might well "find new hope and motivation if their advancement on the job were directly related to part-time study"; 5) The program should "focus heavily on unmet social needs—for example, by building clinics in areas of poverty, which are shockingly short of medical services"; 6) New careers should be developed out of the reconstruction effort itself—clinics should employ "health aides drawn from the community . . . youth should be encouraged to move from construction to the study of architecture." Small business opportunities should arise in building supplies, furniture, markets, restaurants, and so forth. There should be possibilities for artists and musicians; 7) The planning and management of reconstruction projects require a great measure of cooperation among agencies of government and the private sector, but above all local community development corporations must be set up to make sure the projects really belong to the people who live where the needs are. These corporations will be "able to energize the people of the community and control the programs which shape their lives."[20] With such an approach, Kennedy said, would come "leadership willing to see beyond the crisis of today, to the promise and the hope of tomorrow . . . . And we shall have, not rebellion in the streets—but a revolution of freedom within our hearts."[21]

A few days later, campaigning in California, Kennedy spoke of a "national agenda before us." The times called for a new arrangement of the national priorities "so that each of us in his own way, can help to fuse private freedom and public purpose in a new American commonwealth." He went on to offer the same program he had proposed at Gary, but happily buttressed his argument with the announcement that "only this week," the chairman of IBM had agreed to build a new plant in Bedford-Stuyvesant that would create three hundred new jobs.[22]

In the same speech he likened the effort he proposed— "radically new kinds of abilities, to solve awesome problems"—to the effort which had built "an impregnable defense" and had moved the space program forward.

We now spend almost $18 billion on research and development in public funds alone. We have scarcely begun to put this resource to work within our own concerns. Surely this kind of incentive, offered to the men who are building for defense and space can also encourage them to build what we need so desperately within our own cities and communities, so that men will walk on the moon and walk with pride in the streets of American cities.[23]

On occasion Kennedy asserted the priority of jobs over any sort of welfare before audiences not easily persuaded. At a rally in Detroit's John F. Kennedy Square, for example, he opened his speech with words that seemed to challenge the United Automobile Workers, whose support he badly needed, on one of their main demands: "In recent months we have heard a great deal about a guaranteed income. I would rather work for guaranteed jobs and guaranteed training for every American who wants them."[24] The speech went on to suggest improvements in the labor laws and in other social legislation that would be welcome to most union workers. But at the end he went back to the matter of jobs: ". . . most important, we need to create millions of new jobs, especially for those now in poverty." Here was a program "to infuse America with a sense of productive purpose—working together to build a country."[25]

As the primary campaign neared its climax in California —after his victories in Indiana, Nebraska, Washington, D. C. and his loss in Oregon—Kennedy put together all of his major ideas for the cities and the national economy in a series of papers. "A Program for the Urban Crisis," distributed to the press on May 31, discussed in greater detail his proposals for a "special impact program," his recommendations for attracting private investment in reconstruction, and his plan for making low-interest capital available to black businessmen. Further, the paper outlined proposals for revising adult education and training programs, for increasing the mobility of the labor force, for a computerized job bank, reform of the welfare system,* and a program

---

* Kennedy's approach to the welfare problem is discussed in chapter 6, in connection with the policy of the Nixon administration.

both to build great numbers of housing units and to expand home ownership.

But the high points of the paper were the reiteration of two steady themes of the whole campaign: the interrelatedness of all the critical social problems and the dependence of the hope of reducing crime upon building up the society.

As I have stated on many occasions in the past, no program to attack the problems of the inner city can be conducted in the isolation of the ghetto. Our efforts in urban America must be combined with programs to create opportunity for the poor on the farms and in small towns and suburban communities. Jobs, education, health care, housing—all must be provided for the poor wherever they live or want to live.[26]

On crime, the language was even stronger:

There are those who call the poverty areas in our cities "jungles" and refer to them as "brutal societies" which may "annex the affluent suburbs." But the serious and accelerating problem of crime will not be reduced by preying on the legitimate fears of those who are justifiably afraid to walk the streets at night. Over the long run it will be reduced by the building of a society in which people do not want to and do not feel the need to violate the law—a society where equal opportunity for all is a reality, a society where self-respect and self-esteem are not commodities reserved for the economically advantaged.[27]

In the same paper Kennedy underlined his insistence that high-sounding rhetoric must not be allowed to cover inaction. To demand instant integration when integration is impossible on any significant scale is no solution to the race problem. Dispersal of the poor, black or white, from the ghettoes into the suburbs is a hollow slogan:

. . . it must be understood that the building of a truly integrated society depends on the development of economic self-sufficiency and security in the communities of poverty, for only then will the residents of these areas have the wherewithal to move freely within the society. Those who speak of ending the colonialism of the ghetto must therefore recognize that the economic and social development of that community is at the heart of any policy of creating mobility.[28]

The issue arose pointedly on the very next day in Kennedy's nationally televised debate with Senator McCarthy. McCarthy agreed with Kennedy that "industry should be introduced into the slums," but proposed that "some of the inhabitants of the slums be moved to outlying areas." Kennedy, with heavy irony, wanted to know how this would be done "in Orange County." "It would be impractical," he said, "to relocate slum residents now, they would not be able to afford housing, would not be able to compete for jobs, and would find their children unable to meet school standards."[29] Two years later the Nixon administration, as well as many white leaders—both liberal and conservative, Democrats and Republicans—were saying that integration in the inner cities was impractical, and some black leaders were agreeing. But the effort to make it possible was simply not being made, and Bedford-Stuyvesant was at once a kind of forlorn emblem of the hopes that Robert Kennedy had inspired and the possibilities inherent in the kind of presidential leadership he advocated.

FOUR

Youth, Politics, and the Presidency

To anyone old enough to remember the mood and the style of rebellious alienation among German students in the days of the Weimar Republic, and the consequences reaped in 1933 and after, the view across the gulf of generations in the United States in the last third of the twentieth century must be not only puzzling and dismaying but foreboding. The obvious dangers in historical analogizing warn, of course, against prophecy. But the flouting of "law and order," the contempt for "politics," and the unmeasured idealism of German students, countering the preoccupation of their parents and of the Weimar authorities with the security of property and the encouragement of bourgeois virtues, should be instructive to American leaders today, both among young people and among those of their elders who reject and sometimes fear them. Above all, such perspective is indispensable to the President of the United States.

Unhappily this was not the perspective of Richard Nixon's 1968 campaign for President as the champion of "law and order." While Nixon himself was careful not to identify placard-waving demonstrators and long hair with crime or moral degeneracy, he was equally careful not to repudiate his friends and supporters who did. There was in his campaign no suggestion that there could be important justification for youthful rebellion; instead there was a thematic insistence that the rebels were a small minority and that candidate Nixon "had full confidence in the great patriotic majority." It was not surprising that post-election analyses showed that Nixon ran well behind Hubert Humphrey among voters under thirty.

But Humphrey himself failed notably in his appeal to the young. If he was preferable to Nixon in the minds of almost all activist youth except those on the right, he was not attractive, and very large numbers simply decided not to vote at all. His frequent emphasis on his sympathy with youthful radicalism, liberally reenforced with reminders of his own activism as a young man, struck many as merely tiresome. Some, like Tom Hayden, saw in Humphrey's nomination the ultimate bankruptcy of the Democratic party and advocated "direct action" as the only remaining means to significant reform. Others, like Jack Newfield, more restrained but hardly less discouraged, saw Humphrey as a symbol of the very success of Democratic economic and social policies that had resulted in the smugness youth was rejecting. This was hardly fair to Humphrey, who was given no credit for such ideas as the Job Corps, or even the Peace Corps, which he had proposed well before John Kennedy brought it into being. But it is no recent discovery that youth is cruel, and Humphrey must have remembered his own acid denunciation of Southern senators at the Democratic convention of 1948 when he was the "boy mayor" of Minneapolis. At any rate, there was no empathy between Humphrey and the "concerned young Democrats" of 1968. Had there been, he would in all likelihood have won the election.

The case with Eugene McCarthy was, of course, very different. There was no doubt that his appeal to youth was direct, immediate, and effective. Indeed, there is no clear historic parallel to McCarthy's New Hampshire primary campaign, with its political shock troops composed almost wholly of university students, most on leave from their classes and converging on New Hampshire from all parts of the country and by every means of conveyance. "Stay clean for Gene," partly a joke but generally observed, was a poignant expression of the spirit of the campaign. The enthusiasm and dedication of the young amateur politicians were directly reminiscent of the idealism of early Peace Corps volunteers. What they had to give was not skill or experience but energy and devotion to a cause they could believe in. Unkempt appearance and outrageous manners and language are intentional, visible signals of youthful rejection of what is not believed in—and so neatness and good manners and polite language were appropriate to the McCarthy campaign in New Hampshire.

Success in New Hampshire brought thousands more into McCarthy's Pied-Piper-like quest for the Democratic presidential nomination. But neither their numbers nor their enthusiasm ever really had a serious chance to win at Chicago. McCarthy's popularity in the polls was no measure of delegate strength, as Gallup and Harris frequently reminded their readers. Students of politics as well as practitioners were unanimous in their belief that a one-issue campaign (the war) with overemphasis on youth, could only split the convention, confirm the great majority in precisely the "Establishment" posture McCarthy and his followers were attacking, and leave a minority embittered and disillusioned. And so, of course, it happened.

In the primary campaigns the McCarthy forces could not match Robert Kennedy's strength anywhere except in atypical Oregon. After his death they could not understand why so many Kennedy people would not go over to McCarthy. Their own campaign was itself the explanation—aside from the personal magnetism of Robert Kennedy—and reveals a good deal about the politics of presidential leadership.

Before the 1968 campaign actually began, Robert Kennedy's appeal to youth was almost legendary. His close and happy relationship to his own large family, his frequent feats of physical stamina or daring, his outreaching toward the children in his street crowds and in his more formal audiences, his youthful appearance and gait, not to speak of his shaggy hair—all fostered an image of a public man who cared about young people and wished to know them and to listen to them. And, of course, his opposition to the war endeared him to the youth of the peace movement.

There is no doubt that Kennedy drew strength from the response of young people and that he came to depend on them as major constituents of his political representation.

He was hurt deeply that some of the most devoted turned against him when he announced his candidacy after the New Hampshire primary. Eugene McCarthy lost no opportunities to capitalize on Kennedy's late start and often scored heavily with his own youthful supporters by his strokes of irony and scorn. But Kennedy's appeal to the young nevertheless remained far stronger than McCarthy's and reached across a wider spectrum of youthful opinion. The reasons for the defections of some one-time Kennedy followers were a good deal more profound than resentment because he had followed McCarthy into the campaign and refused to offer his support to McCarthy. Below that surface was disillusionment with the very nature of Kennedy's conception of presidential leadership and his campaign posture.

The campaign was based both on his own experience and empathy with young people and his dedication to bringing about such reforms as would win their allegiance not only to the country but to its free politics. There were some young people who simply could not be persuaded. Kennedy had compassion for this " 'underground' community [that] preaches the message of total alienation: 'turn on, tune in, drop out.' " But he saw their life style as "in every way a repudiation of modern American life." He was willing to learn from them what he could, but they represented not hope, not the future, not the betterment of American life, but lack of the nerve that was needed. Fortunately there were not too many of them yet: "These communities are small; but many more young people are sympathetic to the message of estrangement and disillusion even as they reject total alienation."

Kennedy feared that "the premises of the underground are . . . shared by far too many of those young people on whom we depend to commit themselves personally to public change." Nevertheless, it was to those leaders that he directed his appeal:

They seek change, but with an increasing sense of futility: theirs is not the estrangement that leads to complete alienation, but a despair that leads to indifference. Even those young people who are anxious to make a personal effort to alter conditions they oppose, retreat in the face of inflexible institutions with overwhelming power, to become no different from the majority of their generation. These, too, drop out —but by becoming part of the "system" they deplore.[1]

To bring together in a coalition of the young both those still sufficiently moved by idealism to try and those already prepared to give up was Kennedy's purpose. To do it meant that he had to communicate to them his own conviction that "we can do better," and join them with the larger coalition of the poor, the minorities, and the concerned everywhere that would give him a mandate, as President, to "turn this country around."

In *To Seek a Newer World* Kennedy identified at least five leading causes for the disaffection of the young: the war in Vietnam and, in general, the negative policy of anticommunism; the failure of the business system to serve the public interest; hypocrisy in the ethics of their elders; disillusionment with liberal institutions including labor unions; and the inadequacy of the universities.[2]

Vietnam he saw as "a shock" to young people as it could not be to people who had known World War II and the Korean War coming within a space of only a few years. The Vietnam war was "surrounded by a rhetoric they do not accept or understand" because the youth "are the children not of the Cold War, but of the Thaw."

Their memories of Communism are not of Stalin's purges and death camps, not even the terrible revelations of the Twentieth Party Congress, or the streets of Hungary. They see the world as one in which Communist states can be each other's deadliest enemies, or even close to the West, in which Communism is certainly no better, but perhaps no worse, than many other evil and repressive dictatorships with which we conclude alliances when that is felt to be in our interest.

It was not only the distorted perspective on the war itself but the entrapment and the waste that repelled young people, with Kennedy's full sympathy:

We speak of past commitments, of the burden of past mistakes; and they ask why they should now atone for mistakes made before many of them were born, before almost any could vote. They see us spend billions on armaments while poverty and ignorance continue at home;

they see us willing to fight a war for freedom in Vietnam, but
unwilling to fight with one-hundredth the money or force or effort to
secure freedom in Mississippi or Alabama or the ghettoes of the
North. And they see, perhaps most disturbing of all, that they are
remote from the decisions of policy; they themselves do not . . . share
in the power of choice on great questions that shape their lives.

For these reasons it has been tempting in recent years to
blame all or most of the alienation of young people, together with the miseries of the ghetto and social evils in
general, on the war, even on President Johnson personally.
However appealing it may be to find a scapegoat so easily,
the ending of the war will not close the generation gap or
resolve any of the problems that otherwise beset the country. Kennedy, unlike some peace leaders and politicians, was
emphatic on this point: "Nor can this problem," he wrote,
"be traced to any individual, or to any administration, or to
a political party; the challenge is deeper and broader."

Among other identifiable causes for the rebellion of the
young was the fact "that the great corporations that are so
large a part of American life play so small a role in the
solution of its vital problems." Business, Kennedy pointed
out, "with a few important exceptions," had done little to
help meet such "deep crises" as civil rights, poverty, unemployment, and health. If it were argued that the business of
corporations is to make a profit, "that to attempt more is to
do less than its stockholders deserve," such an argument
would have little relevance. What can it mean to young
people in the face of the fact that "a single company, like
General Motors or AT&T, has annual profits greater than
the gross national product of any one of seventy nations in
the world?"

The ethics of profitmaking seem even more unconsciona-
bly hypocritical: "They have seen high officers of the nation's largest corporations engage in conspiracies to fix
prices, gathering in shabby secret meetings to steal pennies a
month from each of millions of Americans." This was strong
language, but Kennedy felt strongly. As Attorney General
and as a Senate committee counsel he had seen at first hand
not only the rise of the juvenile crime rate but just how

shabby the most exalted business leaders could sometimes be.
In betraying themselves and the "system" they were creating outright enemies or, at the least, disgusting the sensitive
and thoughtful young men and women of the new generation. From the perspective of youth almost anything
seemed to be justified by making a profit:

They have seen us send people to jail for the possession of marijuana,
while refusing to limit the sale or advertising of cigarettes, which kill
thousands of Americans each year. [In a footnote Kennedy cited one
tobacco executive who had resigned saying "I guess I just don't think
it's right to make a profit out of killing people."] They have seen us
hesitate to impose the weakest of safety standards on automobiles, or
require that a "respectable" store or lending company tell the simple
truth about the interest rate it is charging on loans.

On top of this indictment must be added the tolerance of
organized crime: ". . . an empire of corruption, venal greed,
and extortion, continues to flourish: not only tolerated, but
often in alliance with significant elements in labor, business,
and government."

The songs of the new generation express their disgust
with crass materialism. "The suburbs are 'little
boxes . . . all made of ticky tacky, and they all look just the
same.'" And "Money can't buy love." In their anger they
"echo the teachings of another rebellious young man: 'The
rich He hath sent empty away.'"

Turning to labor, Kennedy felt compelled to repeat the
charges he had made years before as counsel to the
McClellan committee in the Senate, charges he knew to be
true and disheartening to young people—and not likely to
win votes among trade union leaders who traditionally support Democratic candidates for President. Like the war in
Vietnam it was a matter of experience and perspective.
Older people "have as a frame of reference the long struggle
to establish labor's basic rights, to make the working man
something more than an industrial serf." But to young people, maturing long after those rights had been won,

labor has grown sleek and bureaucratic with power, sometimes
frankly discriminatory, occasionally even corrupt and exploitative, a
force not for change, but for the status quo, unwilling or unable to

organize new members, indifferent to the men who once worked the coal mines of Appalachia, a latecomer to the struggles of the grape pickers of California or the farm laborers of the Mississippi Delta.

This was "a one-sided picture," Kennedy conceded, "without the dimensions of fifty years of struggle, and the undramatic yet vital work of labor in many parts of the nation today." But it was sufficiently accurate nevertheless "for us to be concerned about our children's view, and not to ignore the need for change."

In student rebellion against university administration, faculty, trustees, and custom and in student demands for drastic revision of curriculum and for full-scale participation in decision making, Kennedy saw "a protest of individuality against the university as corporate bureaucracy, against . . . dull sameness." As in the university, so only more so in politics: "the sense that no one is listening." Students and other young people are needed in Peace Corps, in VISTA, and to fight our wars. If they are needed, they had better be heeded.

To the notion, often comfortingly stated, that the young are always rebels and will mature and settle down, Kennedy's response was not calculated to win votes. "The protest of the young," he wrote, "both reflects and worsens their elders' own lack of self-confidence." The trouble, in short, is with American society itself, not just a part of it:

If the young reject a life of corporate bureaucracy and suburban sameness, surely this reflects their parents' dissatisfaction with their own lives, the realization at forty or fifty that money and status have not brought happiness or pride along with them. If the young scorn conventional politics and mock our ideals, surely this mirrors our own sense that these ideals have too often and too easily been abandoned for the sake of comfort and convenience.

The irony is nearly complete:

Most of us can remember, after all, when the aim of youth was to grow into the society of its elders. Now it seems that the young no longer want to exchange their innocence for responsibility; instead many adults seek to recapture childish things.

Kennedy saw in universal education, extending from grade school through high school and finally into the college and graduate years, "an important shift in the nature of modern society." What he called "adolescence"—a somewhat strained use of the term—has intervened between childhood and adulthood, between apprenticeship and station in life, as a kind of station in itself with its own values, customs, and sense of community. Because youth is now an extended time of life, its culture grows ever further apart from that of its elders. There is less and less "continuity of values."

Thus the overriding problem presented by the revolt of the young is to be found not so much in what they believe, in the commitments they make, as in their rejection of any sort of basic agreement "at a time when many others are also denying the fundamental premises and processes of the nation." When the "great gulf" between the young and their elders is added to those between black and white, right and left, rich and poor "there is the danger that too many will not share the same goals, the same understanding of the present or vision of the future." If that happens "our politics and our life will lose much of their capacity to move forward, because we will not agree on where we want to go —or even where we are at the time."

In Kennedy's view such divisions do not promise creative change. In *To Seek a Newer World* he categorically rejected the "politics of confrontation," foreshadowing some of the sharpest and saddest moments of his campaign for the Presidency when he brought down upon his head the wrath of student radicals. It was one thing, and an essential thing, to listen to the young and to empathize with their frustrations and their grievances; it was another, and a mistaken thing, to suppose that the changes borne of confrontation "will be favorable to their aims." The prospects were quite the opposite.

I do not share this blithe confidence. It is undoubtedly healthy for us to confront ourselves and each other, *together*, and with a consciousness of shared aims and good will. But to confront each other across gulfs of hostility and mistrust only invites disaster, as does the intemperate and emotional rejection of general standards of decent speech and behavior.

In a footnote Kennedy quoted a passage from Stillman and Pfaff's *The Politics of Hysteria* on the manner in which the rebels of the twenties and thirties attacked those who "clung to the battered framework of nineteenth-century liberalism, of Enlightenment humanism, of traditional Christianity." These attacks, he noted, were "more than a little reminiscent of some present radical attitudes within the United States."

Thus Kennedy approached a campaign for the Presidency prepared to offer sympathetic leadership to the young, to direct the attention of everyone to the legitimacy of youthful impatience and complaint. Where the young were unwilling to practice the discipline of democracy, he would oppose them, but he would seek to make that discipline worth the price:

Whatever their differences with us, whatever the depth of their dissent, it is vital for us as much as for them that our young feel that change is possible, that they will be heard, that the follies and cruelties of the world will yield, however grudgingly, to the sacrifices they are prepared to make. Above all, we seek a sense of possibility.

The issues of the campaign itself were not "young" issues or "old" issues but more like perennial issues not willing to be put off much longer. For a candidate with Kennedy's sense of urgent need for a strong Presidency, the political problem was to persuade young people that bad or ineffective policies are reversible within the American system while, at the same time, not contributing for his own part to the generation gap he hoped to bridge. Because, as President, he wanted a mandate not only to end the war but to end poverty and discrimination and crime by the radical means he believed necessary, he could not build majority support without concurrently building a measure of minority opposition. This principle held true of youth as well as of any other segment of American society. Just as the President cannot cater to youth without alienating at least some of their elders, so he cannot appeal to some young people without offending others. The candidate who seeks to avoid the dilemma by offending nobody, except perhaps numerically insignificant minorities, may succeed in winning an election, but he does not thereby escape the problems demanding to be resolved. Conversely, a candidate's best hope to control and shape social change is to build a majority behind his program by appealing to any who will listen, white or black, rich or poor, young or old. This was the point of Kennedy's approach to youth in 1968.

At the outset of his campaign, Kennedy told the students of the University of Alabama that he would not "paper over our differences on specific issues." He would appeal to them—a presumably hostile audience—because he believed that his differences with them were not so great as "the principles which unite us." Those principles were, he hoped, a shared belief in the processes of free government and a determination to make them work:

> The gulf between our people will not be bridged by those who preach violence, or by those who burn and loot. I run for President because I believe such anarchy is intolerable—and I want to do something about it. But I also run because I believe that these divisions will not be solved by demagogues—by men who seek power by preaching suspicion and mistrust—or by those who would meet legitimate grievances with the heavy hand of repression . . . . I run for President because I want to do something about violence in our streets. But I also run because I want citizens to have an equal chance for jobs and decent housing.[3]

Some followers of George Wallace left early, but the all-white audience greatly outcheered the hecklers.

A few days later Kennedy stated his position even more explicitly in California before the students of San Fernando Valley State College:

> I am on the side of those who seek to bring jobs into the dark corners of our nation—in city slum and rural hollow—where proud men seek work and receive a welfare handout. I am with those who seek to build their communities instead of ignoring them out of apathy, or destroying them out of despair.
>
> I am on the side of those who seek more than blind dissent, and who respect the opinions of others. I am with those who express not simply opposition to the present, but propositions for the building of a better country.

There were already rumbles of displeasure in the crowd, and the next words increased the volume of heckling and cheering: "I am on the side of those who do not shout down others; but who listen, challenge, and then propose a better policy for America."[4]

As the weeks went by and Kennedy visited many colleges the response was always the same. The majority of the students, usually the great majority, gave him their enthusiasm—though some were supporters of McCarthy. But articulate minorities did not hesitate to heckle whenever he affirmed his faith in politics or the responsibilities of citizenship. Occasionally, as at a rally in Denver, he defied their sensibilities by including their parents in the future.

Young people have a great contribution to make. But it cannot be an exclusive contribution. It must be shared not only by white Americans, but by black Americans, seeking a new direction and a new dignity. It must be shared not only by students, or those with college educations, but also by those who did not have the opportunity to attend college. It must be shared not only by the young, but also by your parents, and those of even greater age; for though they may have fewer years remaining than youth, their desires for the future of their children and grandchildren are as deep as ours for our own.[5]

Kennedy's speeches to young people were in most respects similar to those he gave before open political rallies and meetings. He outlined his stand on the war and his proposals for peace, asked support for his attack on poverty and the decay of the cities, and pleaded for reconciliation among the races. But his manner was to speak directly to the young and to emphasize the role he hoped they would play, and to let them know unmistakably that he thought they ought to play it. Sometimes he cut his talks short in order to give the time to questions. Often the ensuing dialogue would be more effective than a formal address could ever be. More than once, for example, skeptical students asked him, "Who is going to pay for all this?" "You are," he would tell them. If some were nettled, more were delighted by sallies of this sort.

But the all-pervasive topic in these meetings with students was the war. And it was the war that most sharply revealed the dimensions of the problem Kennedy sought to resolve. For unfriendly voices were heard from many more than just a few hecklers. At the University of San Francisco, indeed, he was shouted down and could not deliver his prepared address at all. Going directly to questions, he carried a majority with him. But the going was very uncertain.

On such occasions he answered questions in sober, sometimes deadly earnest. "Senator, if you are so against the war, would you, as President, pardon draft resisters?" "No, I would not." "If you were our age, Senator, what would you do if you were called to military service?" "I would serve." These were not popular answers. But Kennedy tried to explain to those who would listen that the President of the United States could not honorably use his power of pardon to contravene the laws of the nation. He believed in national service. To protest, to demonstrate, to seek redress by petition, to change the law or the policy by electing men with different views, even to go to jail for conscience—all were proper, perhaps desirable; but the President could not, and he would not if elected, tolerate obstruction contrary to law.

At Oregon State University Kennedy outlined a specific plan for "alternative service" and asked the young people to support it. It was a plan he advocated before many audiences around the country. Pleading with students to plan for a period of service at the outset of their adult lives, he sought to show them how they could "become critical links" in new organizations to "place control over policy and resources directly into the hands of those who use them" in attacking social problems:

. . . as doctors, you can work in Neighborhood Health Centers bringing medical care back from impersonal overworked hospitals, trying to train unemployed people as health aides . . . .
. . . as lawyers, you can work with Neighborhood Assemblies, where citizens once again gain a direct voice in the affairs of their own government . . . .
. . . as teachers, you can help staff new kinds of schools . . . bringing new kinds of educational techniques to the task of teaching children to learn and think for themselves . . . .

. . . as engineers and technicians, you can help direct the rebuilding of urban and rural America, giving to the jobless not welfare, but employment; designing new materials and new techniques for efficient use of the funds we have.[6]

In exchange for such commitments, he proposed to revise the draft law: "In brief, I believe that if the difficulties could be resolved this government ought to discharge young men from their military obligations if they have given a different, but equally valuable kind of service to their country."

This proposal, previously suggested by Robert McNamara and others, was well received at Oregon State and elsewhere. But the words of caution he always added tended to dampen enthusiasm and often provoked a round of heckling:

Let me be clear: I do not come here promising to develop a quick system of alternative service to the draft. There are serious difficulties involved in any such attempt:

It could work only in peacetime. For nothing is comparable to the risk of combat; and those burdens must be shared by all.

It could not be allowed to reinforce the social and economic disparity already rampant in our system of service. Clearly, alternative service would have to be open to all, including those who lacked the chance to go on to college and develop skills.

So I do not come before you with an easy answer . . . I say that even as we honor those who fight to defend this nation, we should honor those who work to improve the quality of our national life . . . .[7]

In all his encounters with young audiences on university campuses and elsewhere, Kennedy went away with the support of what appeared to be the majority, and with the respect of almost all for his conception of the national future and the role he was asking young people to play. That role involved idealistic commitment and hard work. But it was not romantic or spectacular. Kennedy often used sentences from his book to underscore the point: "When Rap Brown threatens to 'burn America down,' he is not a revolutionary, he is an anarchist. The end is not a better life for black people; it is a devastated America." That "program for death, not life" must be "met with the full force of the law."

But it was "necessary to look beyond suppression, and beyond law enforcement." Students, and their elders, must stop thinking of the "young man of the ghetto . . . as a liability . . . . Let us think of him instead as a valuable resource." From this perspective, the privileged youth of the universities could join with the poor not only of their own age but of any age and of any color in the effort to rebuild the nation.

The risks in this kind of campaign, even for a candidate with a headstart of unusual appeal for young people, are great. To some the proposals are not radical enough; to others they are utopian. Because the proposals do not promise immediate results, many people are impatient. And because they not only rely upon but pointedly advocate the free politics of the "system" the would-be revolutionary enemies of the "system" will scoff. Such proposals, in short, cannot unite the youth of the nation any more than a radical and expensive attack on urban poverty and discrimination can unite all the people of the ghettoes with those of the suburbs.

But the American presidential system does not rest upon unity of support for program and policy. It rests upon agreement as to the means of adopting program and policy. If there is a clear majority for measures the President advocates, and if those measures are within the resources of the nation, the Congress, perhaps not without quarrelsome resistance, will enact whatever laws are necessary and the measures will be carried out. Kennedy's encounter with youth in 1968, quite aside from its qualities of drama, was an effort, necessary to the presidential system itself, to attach as many young people as he could to the coalition he hoped to build into a majority behind his leadership and his program. Without young people in it and behind it a President's program cannot significantly build for the future, as President Nixon quickly discovered. It can only move toward national disaster, or perhaps temporize for a time—which is really a slower way of moving in the same direction.

PART II

Afterwards

Roosevelt once told us that the system of party responsibility in America requires a . . . liberal party and a conservative party, and so it is today. We have no need —indeed, we cannot afford—to blur distinctions and eliminate differences, until the people are left with no dialogue and no choice except the pleasure of a candidate's smile.

—ROBERT F. KENNEDY

FIVE

Presidential Politics

It goes without saying that politics is an indispensable ingredient of leadership. But in the present era of American experience, survival of the presidential system may depend upon the degree to which Presidents and presidential candidates succeed in subordinating the craft of politics to the purpose of productive leadership. If a distinction between *presidential politics* and the *politics of presidential leadership* appears at first sight arbitrary, or at least elusive, it is nonetheless essential to make such a distinction.

For the purpose here, *presidential politics* means manipulation of the power and influence of the presidential office to achieve undeclared objectives or to avoid, or at least to diminish, the necessity of making choices of policy and program which would induce change not desired by the President or sufficiently divisive to threaten the degree of "nonpartisan" popularity to which he may aspire. For a presidential candidate, it means avoiding or "strategically obfuscating" divisive issues. An important variant of this proposition is that presidential politics may, upon occasion, mean manipulation of presidential power and influence to give the appearance of pursuing a course other than the course actually being pursued. Further, not to indulge in the pleasantly partisan game of attributing lofty or else mean and merely selfish motives to the President, the discussion here presumes that he practices presidential politics because he deems it in the best interest of the nation to do so. Several instances, to be examined presently, will illustrate both the means and the ends in view.

The *politics of presidential leadership*, subject of the next chapter, means manipulation of the power and influence of

87

the presidential office—or a candidate's proposal to do so —to secure popular and congressional support for declared policies and programs which are necessarily to a significant degree divisive because addressed to the resolution of problems arising in part from the existence of division. *Note that the less division there is, the less is the problem of leadership a political problem.* If the choice to be made is seriously divisive, this proposition entails the risk of loss of prestige and perhaps of power itself should a sufficient body of support not be forthcoming. For a presidential candidate, of course, the risk is loss of the election. Again, apart from idiosyncratic motives, the presumption is that the President or presidential candidate makes and advocates choices of divisive program and policy because he deems it in the national interest to do so. It must be added, as corollary, that a President otherwise inclined to vigorous leadership may, wisely, refrain from such action when, in his judgment, the probability of success must be discounted by certainty that failure would incur unacceptable loss of prestige to his office and thus impair his ability to govern effectively.

Franklin D. Roosevelt and Richard Nixon had little in common in matters of policy or program. But their express conceptions of presidential leadership were parallel, and both were addicted to the use of presidential politics. In one matter in particular they would, surprisingly, have found a substantial measure of agreement: arranging a Supreme Court to their liking. In both cases the means used were those of political manipulation as opposed to political leadership.

In the campaign of 1936 the Democrats had frequently criticized the Supreme Court for the flow of adverse decisions which had invalidated some important New Deal measures, though not so many as legend has it. Roosevelt himself had spoken disparagingly of the "Nine Old Men" and their persistence in "the horse and buggy age." But neither the Democratic platform nor the campaign speeches of the President had suggested a purpose to pack the Court with pro-New Deal judges. Thus the President's proposal, sent to Congress on February 5, 1937, was received with surprise and dismay.

Much of the plan had to do with the lower courts. But the crucial provision was to permit retirement of Supreme Court judges at age seventy on full salary, and to allow the President to appoint an additional justice to the Court for each justice who elected not to retire, up to a total membership of fifteen as against the statutory nine. Since the four leading Court opponents of Roosevelt's program were all over seventy, the President could by this means immediately secure a majority in his favor.

In the plan itself, and in the early stages of promoting it, emphasis was placed solely on obtaining greater efficiency and speeding up the work of the Court. In response to the charge that he was "Court packing," Roosevelt spoke with righteous indignation about the integrity of judges and his belief in the separation of powers. But as the battle raged —and rage it did, in the Congress and in public debate—the issue narrowed to the question whether the President had a mandate to carry on and perfect a program endorsed overwhelmingly by the electorate but possible, according to Roosevelt, only by a change in the Supreme Court.

Roosevelt's appeal, in a radio "fireside chat" and in numerous statements at press conferences, was to this presumed mandate. The appeal was disingenuous, since he had at no time asked for support in a reorganization of the Court. Yet the popularity of his measures and of his leadership had certainly been demonstrated in the election. In the end the President, in defeat, discovered that his mandate did not extend to radical measures of government overhaul which he had deliberately avoided discussing in the campaign. The Supreme Court—his opponents insisted that it was the Constitution itself at issue—was "sacred," which was no doubt why he had not attacked it directly in the campaign. At any rate his political ploy failed, with serious consequences thereafter for his leadership in domestic affairs. His efforts to "purge" some of his congressional opponents in the Democratic primaries of 1938 were all rebuffed. And in the election his margins in both houses were so reduced that the old "coalition" of Republicans and conservative Democrats, routed in 1936, returned to power.[1]

There is, of course, no strict parallel between Roosevelt's battle with the Supreme Court and Richard Nixon's 1970 battle with the Senate about the Supreme Court. But the ends in view were the same, at least in part, and the means employed in both cases was certainly presidential politics.

In seeking a nominee for a second vacancy on the Court, after the well-received nomination of Warren Burger to be Chief Justice, President Nixon had two major concerns, the one openly stated, the other well understood but not stated. In the first instance, he was anxious to add a justice whose views were "strict constructionist," like his own. In the second, he wished to nominate a Southern judge whose appointment would please the growing body of Southern politicians in both parties who looked to him for help in slowing down the rate of desegregation and, in general, reasserting the presumed rights of the states against constitutional decisions of the Supreme Court.

Each of Nixon's nominations, first, Judge Clement Haynsworth and second, Judge G. Harrold Carswell, was intended to achieve both purposes. Both men were known as conservative or "strict constructionist" judges on the Circuit Court bench, and both were Southerners. The reasons given by the opposition senators, who succeeded in defeating both nominees, differed in certain respects. Haynsworth was held to have violated ethical canons by sitting in judgment of cases where he had an interest, while Carswell was held to be intellectually unfit. In both cases there was a strong feeling and some evidence that the nominees were not in sympathy with the established rules of the Supreme Court on racial segregation, but Carswell was shown to have been in his youth a white supremacist and while on the bench to have given evidences of continuing prejudice. However, the reasons for rejection are less to the point here than the President's reasons for the nominations and his efforts to have them confirmed.

President Nixon claimed a mandate to appoint a strict constructionist to the Supreme Court. In the campaign of

1968 he had often spoken of his belief that the Court had "bent over too far backward" in its decisions protecting the rights of persons under criminal prosecution. To try to tighten up the judicial system by adding judges who were prepared to show greater concern for public order and the reduction of crime than he believed had been true of the Warren Court was a central part of his promise to restore "law and order." There is no doubt that this position was widely appealing, not only to those who declared themselves conservatives but to many of those Nixon liked to call "the silent majority."

It may be thought querulous by some to inquire whether Nixon's election gave him the mandate he claimed. But the meaning of presidential leadership and its fitness to meet the crises of this era depend upon just such inquiries. If it is assumed, which seems safe enough, that the Wallace voters agreed with Nixon on the appointment of conservative judges to alter the balance of the Supreme Court and if the Wallace vote is then added to the Nixon vote, a substantial majority can be counted behind the President's promised effort to do so. There can be no effective rebuttal to the contention that the President had a right to interpret the election as strong support for his nomination of strict constructionist judges. It is important to observe that no senators questioned either nomination on this ground.

What was much less clear from the election returns, however, was whether there was a majority for interpreting "strict construction" to include a change in the posture of the Court not only toward criminal law enforcement but toward segregation and discrimination as well. It might be conceded that most or all of the Wallace vote was at least for a "slowdown," but there is no evidence that most of the Nixon voters were saying the same thing. Indeed, there is reason to believe that a good many people voted for Nixon precisely because, though they held more conservative views then Humphrey, they were not prepared to make an effort to resist social change by supporting a demagogic candidate like Wallace. Instead, they accepted Nixon's declaration on racial equality and his slogan of "going forward together."

In view of Hubert Humphrey's lifelong identification with the cause of civil rights, there can hardly have been a significant number of his supporters who wished to alter the nation's course against discrimination. Thus it appears that a substantial majority of the voters in 1968 were actually opposed to reviving the question of discrimination as a constitutional matter. This, at any rate, was the interpretation of the Senate in its inquiry into the fitness of Haynsworth and Carswell.

Why, then did President Nixon make two attempts to put a Southerner with a background in the culture of segregation on the Supreme Court? The historic case of Hugo Black—an Alabaman and one time Klansman who became a leading liberal justice—suggests that to actually change the Court's attitude toward segregation can hardly have been a prime objective. There is, of course, no way of knowing how either Haynsworth or Carswell as Supreme Court justices would have voted on segregation matters. Even their occasional decisions regarded as unfriendly to vigorous enforcement of desegregation could not be cited as evidence of what they would do under the very different conditions that prevail in the Supreme Court.

On the other hand, as the defense of these nominations in the Senate makes clear, there is no doubt that Southern politicians of both parties looked upon them as potential "friends in court." Thus the impression made upon the South appears to have been a prime objective of the President's politics. His debt to some Southern leaders for help in obtaining the nomination at Miami in 1968 was written large in the record of the Republican convention. His hope to win back from Wallace in 1972 the states he had carried in 1960 against Kennedy but lost in 1968, had led to what was widely known as a "Southern strategy" in his whole conception of presidential politics. If there were any doubt on this score, Nixon removed it by his statement after the defeat of Carswell. He attacked the Senate majority, led by Northern Democrats and liberal Republicans, in very tough language. The two nominees, he said, had had "the misfortune" to be born in the South. He would not subject another Southern judge to "the kind of malicious character assassination accorded both Judges Haynsworth and Carswell." He asserted flatly that he would now proceed to nominate a Northern man because the Senate would not confirm a Southerner under any circumstances—an evident inaccuracy and an unaccountable personal insult to such Old Confederacy senators as Fulbright, Yarborough, and Gore, whose votes had in fact defeated Carswell. The President called the criticisms of his two nominees on the score of ethical deficiency or incompetence "hypocritical." Finally, he said: "I understand the bitter feeling of millions of Americans who live in the South about the act of regional discrimination that took place in the Senate yesterday. They have my assurance that the day will come when men like Judges Haynsworth and Carswell will sit on the High Court."[2]

One must share Richard Rovere's inability "to recall any presidential statement in this century as intemperate and as divisive" as this one.[3] The "South" was identified implicitly as white and segregationist, and the President did not hesitate to divide white from black all over the nation.

But the statement was no doubt well directed to the political purpose. The President appeared to the "South" as a friend tried in battle, at the same time that his eventual successful appointee would be from the North and, though perhaps a "strict constructionist," a judge of impeccable character and real distinction. The effort to build a new majority of Republicans and Southern Democratic politicians was advanced, while the "liberals" appeared to the "silent majority" of ordinary citizens as mean obstructionists. That black leaders, and followers, were dismayed was not significant, since their views were not within the scope of the political purpose to be accomplished. If it was objected that the Supreme Court had been "politicized," as the *New York Times* complained, it was fair to ask whether the Court is not always to some degree involved in politics and to remember that many Presidents have involved the Court in presidential politics. Thomas Jefferson's effort to impeach Justice Chase and Roosevelt's effort to pack the Supreme Court are only the most dramatic instances.

Judicial appointments at various levels have always played an important political role. President Kennedy—advised and assisted by his brother as Attorney General—used them to reward his friends and even to punish his enemies. James Doyle, later to become a federal district judge in Wisconsin, was punished by the Kennedys by being denied a seat on the bench when he was first put forward in 1961. His crime was that he had played a leading role in the abortive effort to draft Adlai Stevenson for the Democratic presidential nomination in 1960. While President Kennedy appointed most of the Stevenson leaders to high positions, Robert Kennedy flatly refused to recommend Doyle, despite his unquestioned competence. Someone, in short, had to be sacrificed in the game of presidential politics. That it was in this case a game is indicated by the Attorney General's broad hint that Doyle's exile would not be permanent—as, indeed, it was not.

The most celebrated case of Kennedy politics with a judicial appointment was that of Francis X. Morrissey, a Massachusetts Democratic wheelhorse who had served the Kennedy cause long and faithfully. In 1961 President Kennedy intended to appoint Morrissey to the district court but changed his mind when several Massachusetts bar association committees declared him unfit. Later, when he was leaving office, Attorney General Robert Kennedy asked President Johnson, as a personal political favor, to appoint Morrissey. Johnson did so, but the Senate balked. Despite the vigorous efforts of Senator Edward Kennedy, Morrissey could not be confirmed.

In such cases as these, however, it is important to note that the Supreme Court was not involved. Like his predecessor, President Eisenhower, John Kennedy was careful to send up for the Supreme Court only men of fine reputation and unquestioned legal ability who would increase, not diminish, the Court's stature and prestige. Justice Byron White, a long-time personal friend of President Kennedy, was a distinguished lawyer who had played a leading part in the campaign of 1960 and had served initially as Deputy Attorney General under Robert Kennedy. There was no opposition to his elevation to the Court. As a member of the Court, Justice White in fact tended to adopt a more conservative position than might have been expected of a Kennedy appointee. The appointment of Labor Secretary Arthur Goldberg, who had been General Counsel to the AFL-CIO before 1961, was intended to dramatize President Kennedy's belief that the Brandeis, Cardozo, Frankfurter tradition on the Court ought to be preserved. Though there were no doubt political advantages to President Kennedy in both appointments, it was clear that, unlike Roosevelt and Nixon, he had no intention of trying to shape the political or legal philosophy of the Supreme Court.

Roosevelt's attempt to pack the Supreme Court resulted in the only important political defeat of his Presidency. Though that defeat had serious consequences, his supporters could, nevertheless, argue that his purpose had been to make possible government action which had been endorsed by the electorate. He himself believed that he had "lost a battle, but won the war," since Chief Justice Hughes, acting to defend the Court, moved to swing the majority toward acceptance of the New Deal. The consequences of President Nixon's attempt at making presidential politics with the High Court may not be clear for some time to come. But his claim that opposition to the Haynsworth and Carswell nominations was obstruction of presidential prerogative was neither theoretically justifiable nor well directed to maintaining effective political relations with the Senate.

When President Roosevelt attacked personally the Democratic opponents of his Court plan the voters rebuked him in the primary elections. The political consequences of President Nixon's battle over Supreme Court nominees might be less painful to him. But it was unhappily evident from the outset that he was not only risking the stature of the Court but demeaning the Presidency itself at a critical moment in the history of the Republic. With the judiciary and the executive system under intensifying attack both from the

left and the right, the President raised disquieting questions
in almost everybody's mind.

The problem of race which, together with poverty, Robert Kennedy saw as the most critical and fateful of this era,
reveals better than any other the actual and potential weak-
nesses and strengths of the presidential system. Most Presidents have played politics with it; few have provided anything like effective leadership. Theodore Roosevelt, for
example, cultivated Southern blacks who might be delegates
to Republican national conventions, but yielded to pressures
from Southern whites and withdrew a White House dinner
invitation to Booker T. Washington.

Woodrow Wilson's liberalism did not extend to a
concern for racial equality; nor did Franklin Roosevelt's.
The latter won immense support from blacks, both Northern and Southern, because the social legislation of the New
Deal barred discrimination and assisted black Americans to
improve their economic condition more rapidly than at any
time in history. But he had little taste for fights with Southern Democrats over political or social equality. Even during
World War II, when Adlai Stevenson, as assistant to the
Secretary of the Navy, proposed to eliminate discrimination
among enlisted sailors, arguing that the war itself was being
fought against racism, Roosevelt was merely amused at
such naïveté. The Navy, he told Stevenson, dominated by
Southern officers, would never agree—as though that settled
the matter. Fortunately Stevenson, backed by Secretary
Frank Knox, persisted, and a beginning at desegregation of
the armed forces was made. In contrast to Roosevelt, Harry
Truman, who had much to gain by political accommoda-
tion on the race issue, chose instead to risk the election of
1948 on a strong civil rights plank, the first in either party
after the Compromise of 1877.

In more recent years presidential politics has alternated
with presidential leadership in the field of race relations—
sometimes in the same administration. Dwight Eisenhower
as a candidate carefully avoided discussion of civil rights. As
President, faced with the first revolutionary decisions of the

Supreme Court ordering desegregation of the public schools, he vacillated and equivocated as a matter of policy. He refused to say whether he agreed with the Court's rulings, thus suggesting that he did not. He would simply do his constitutional duty. He refused to take issue with Southern members of Congress who signed a manifesto supporting "interposition" of state authority between the schools and the Supreme Court, declaring, curiously, that "there are adequate legal means of determining all these factors." He refused even to call a conference of Southern leaders to discuss implementation of the Court's decrees. When events forced him to send troops into Little Rock, in September 1957, he explained to the nation that he was doing so only to enforce the law and again displayed his sympathy, if not agreement, with people who opposed desegregation. This consistent posture enabled him to retain the support of Southern politicians and to carry five states of the Old Confederacy. The consequences for his successors and for the nation were, unhappily, a good deal less satisfactory.[4]

John Kennedy, as a candidate in 1960, sought to maintain a strong position on civil rights without offending the South by demanding civil rights legislation. Instead, he attacked the Eisenhower administration for failing to use existing executive authority to eliminate discrimination and promised to make full use of it himself. In particular, he pledged to eliminate by executive order discrimination in federally supported housing. This somewhat ambiguous posture was dictated in part by his fear that his Catholicism was already a sufficiently great handicap in the Southern states, and in part by his judgment that the next Congress would not, in any case, be likely to pass strong civil rights legislation. As politics, John Kennedy's campaign, in this respect, was a failure, since Nixon held the five Southern states that had gone for Eisenhower and added another. As leadership, his campaign handling of the race issue, despite his dramatic intervention to free Martin Luther King from jail, was equally unproductive. He neither won the larger majorities he might have gained in states outside the South by pledging to work for civil rights legislation, nor helped congressional candidates running on strong civil rights pledges, nor won for himself as President a mandate to give leadership to Congress. Kennedy could, however, consistent with his campaign proposals, give vigorous support to the effort to desegregate schools and colleges. Attorney General Robert Kennedy, with the full support of his brother, used every power available for the purpose. In 1963, forced by events to take the political risk of asking for radical civil rights legislation, Robert Kennedy supervised the drawing up of the bill for which President Kennedy was fighting at the time of his death.

Lyndon Johnson took up the cause of civil rights and gave it unprecedented presidential leadership. Going directly to the Congress and the people, he sought and won massive support for the Kennedy civil rights bill, and then went on in the 1964 campaign and afterwards to give decisive leadership toward enactment of laws in the fields of voting and open housing. At the time of his retirement from the 1968 campaign, forward momentum in civil rights was being challenged, from one side, by black militants who maintained that political rights were a sham unless matched by economic and social equality, and, from the other, by growing numbers of whites who felt, apprehensively, that "things were going too far." Nevertheless, the powers of the President as Johnson left them were adequate to continue the movement toward full-scale racial equality.

But almost from the outset the Nixon administration showed reluctance to use the powers available and, in the field of voting, even favored some diminution. Before the end of its first year in office Richard Harris had written a series of articles documenting delays, equivocations, and occasional outright refusals to act by President Nixon's Department of Justice.[5] In the winter of 1969–1970 the Health, Education, and Welfare Department officials responsible for enforcing the Civil Rights Act of 1964 were eased out. In their wake lawyers in unprecedented numbers signed letters of protest or resigned from that department and from the Department of Justice with the complaint that they were not permitted to enforce the law. At the same time there were frequent reports that the Secretary of Health, Education, and Welfare, Robert Finch, and Attorney General John Mitchell were unable to agree on a policy of enforcement of the civil rights laws. Because Mitchell had been Nixon's campaign manager in 1968 and had continued as his chief political adviser, a good deal of opposition criticism was directed at him rather than at Finch. Finally both Finch and his Commissioner of Education, James Allen, were removed from positions of responsibility: Finch to the White House staff and Allen to private life. A year later the erosion was continuing as legal services in the antipoverty programs, often needed in civil rights matters, were sharply reduced.

Richard Nixon had never given more than minimal support either to civil rights decisions of the Supreme Court or to congressional enactments. He had, as Vice President and as a presidential candidate in both 1960 and 1968, stated his agreement with the 1954 Court decision in *Brown* v. *Board of Education*, the leading case on school segregation, and he had often asserted his commitment to equality of opportunity. But he had offered no specific proposals, made no appeal to blacks or other minorities affected, and had actively sought the support of segregationist Southern politicians. He sought no mandate, and on becoming President in 1969 he had none. Like Eisenhower, he had nevertheless the duty to enforce the law and responsibility for national leadership under increasingly tense circumstances.

For many months President Nixon was content to allow Secretary Finch and Attorney General Mitchell to act as administration spokesmen on civil rights in general and school segregation in particular. But the accumulation of lower federal court decisions ordering immediate desegregation, the need for policy in cases of noncompliance with HEW requirements for eligibility for federal assistance, and the hotly disputed matter of busing to achieve integration led him to issue, on March 24, 1970, a detailed and comprehensive statement of policy on the school question.

At first glance the Nixon statement seemed to place him squarely on the side of effective law enforcement and to offer presidential leadership in what he called "America's historic commitment to the achievement of a free and open society." The sheer bulk of the document—some nine thousand words—was impressive. At the beginning he reaffirmed his "personal belief that the 1954 decision of the Supreme Court in *Brown* v. *Board of Education* was right in both constitutional and human terms." He promised that his administration would not back away: "the constitutional mandate will be enforced."[6] But on closer scrutiny—and the statement was inevitably scrutinized with rapt attention by all parties—there turned out to be clusters of calculated ambiguities and some crucial omissions. The conclusion was inescapable that President Nixon was employing that variant of presidential politics which consists of appearing to be following one course while in fact pursuing another.

A central emphasis in President Nixon's statement was on such phrases as "separated by law" and "State-imposed segregation." The President agreed entirely with the *Brown* decision that segregated education is inherently unequal, but he then gave the impression that because de facto segregation was not covered by *Brown* it was not necessary to oppose it. By some legerdemain, segregated education thus became unequal under one set of circumstances but not under another. There followed the argument that the government need not require busing to achieve desegregation of de facto segregated schools. The President stated categorically his "opposition to any compulsory busing of pupils beyond normal geographic school zones for the purpose of achieving racial balance."

At one point Nixon accepted as authoritative and binding a ruling of the Supreme Court that "the obligation of every school district is to terminate dual systems at once and to operate now and hereafter only unitary schools." But later he propounded a doctrine which is hardly compatible with the plain sense of this ruling, whatever may be the legal hairsplitting developed by its opponents:

Racial imbalance in a school system may be partly *de jure* in origin and partly *de facto*. In such a case it is appropriate to insist on a remedy for the *de jure* portion, which is unlawful, without insisting on a remedy for the lawful *de facto* portion.

From the point of view of the pupils and parents in such a "system" the logic of this statement may well have been less impressive than the contrast between equal and unequal education thus sanctioned.

On the other hand, when he proposed "an innovative approach" to education of pupils in city ghettoes, Nixon seemed to accept the proposition that segregated education has undesirable social consequences. The passage is remarkable both for what it suggested and for what it omitted:

. . . rather than attempting dislocation of whole schools, a portion of a child's educational activities may be shared with children from other schools. Some of his education is in a "home base," but some outside it. This "outside learning" is in settings that are defined neither as black nor white and sometimes in settings that are not even in traditional school buildings. It may range all the way from intensive work in reading to training in technical skills and to joint efforts such as drama and athletics.

By bringing the children together on "neutral" territory, friction may be dispelled; by limiting it to part-time activities, no one would be deprived of his own neighborhood school, and the activities themselves provide the children with better education.

Implicit is the notion that there are advantages, not otherwise possible, to be obtained by integration. How such a plan was to be achieved without busing, however, was not considered, presumably because it would have been awkward to assert that busing is appropriate for part-time but not for full-time integration! That children would not "be deprived of their own neighborhood schools" no doubt reassured white suburbia but was received with somewhat less enthusiasm in the ghettoes.

Another theme of the President's statement was a tenuous distinction between *desegregation* and *integration*. For example, he quoted the Court's definition of a "unitary system" as one "within which no person is to be effectively excluded from any school because of race or color." But from this he seemed to draw the conclusion that the Court had "not spoken definitely on whether or not—or the extent to which—'desegregation' may mean 'integration.'"

One is tempted to ask why the Court should go further than it had already gone, and why wait, in any case? The President was content to repeat the assertion that he was "dedicated to continued progress toward a truly desegregated public school system," an assertion which no more carried a definition of "truly desegregated" than did the rulings of the Supreme Court.

By the test of policy laid down as against principle vaguely asserted, it appears that the President was not concerned to act against segregated schools in the ghettoes, or in the South if the cause of segregation was "geographical," and did not believe he was obligated to do so. Instead, he proposed to spend $500 million to improve ghetto schools —"racially impacted areas." In the following fiscal year he increased this sum to a billion. It would be churlish to quarrel with any serious effort to upgrade poor schools anywhere in the country. But the measure of this plan is revealed in the President's own words: The money "must come from other programs. Inevitably, it represents a further reordering of priorities on the domestic scene." It soon developed that the funds were to come from Model Cities, antipoverty, and urban renewal programs.

Thus, reduced to its essentials, the Nixon policy was to enforce only such lower-court orders and executive rulings as apply to school districts where segregation exists by state law or school board intent ("good faith" accepted as evidence of compliance), to refuse to require busing, to initiate part-time integration programs which would require busing, to oppose all segregation but to leave de facto segregation alone, and to assign additional sums of money for the improvement of ghetto schools at the expense of programs to reconstruct the ghettoes that contain them.

Perhaps the most significant aspect of the Nixon statement was not the ambiguous policy he set forth, but the critical question he left out. Nowhere did he mention the Civil Rights Act of 1964. Yet it is this law which provides that federally supported facilities maintaining segregation, including schools, shall be denied funds. And it is this provision that has been the real source of trouble with Southern politicians and their anti-integration followers. By omitting mention of it, Nixon was able to concentrate his attention on an assortment of sometimes contradictory lower-court rulings, holding rightly that there were a number of questions not yet resolved by the Supreme Court. The reader can sympathize with the difficulties the President and his colleagues were facing under such circumstances. It is only when one recollects their obligation to enforce the Civil Rights Act that one discovers that the full effect of the President's discussion was to divert attention from that obligation. Indeed, it was the administration's unwillingness to enforce that law which led to the protests and resignations of civil rights lawyers from the government.

The conclusion from the document itself must be that the President wished to slow down the course toward integration wherever he legally and constitutionally could, while giving the appearance of "dedication" to its advancement. Like the nominations of Judges Haynsworth and Carswell, this brand of presidential politics would be pleasing to segregationist Southern politicians as well as to residual anti-black prejudice wherever it persisted in the South. But the plan was calculated equally to appeal to the large numbers of people outside the South who, according to opinion polls, overwhelmingly oppose mandatory busing, and to the indeterminate number who are apprehensive about possible black emigration from the ghettoes. Read with care, the statement on segregation and the schools explains better than any commentary, however well informed, why President Nixon was willing to quarrel with the Senate over his nominees to the Court yet had no comment on the behavior of a governor of Florida who was at the same moment obstructing and defying integration orders of a federal court. With due recognition of the immense complexity and excruciating difficulty of the school crisis, it is nevertheless plain to see that the prestige of the Presidency cannot be upheld nor the progress of the nation advanced by this kind of diversionary and equivocal presidential politics.

The President's position was roughly shaken by the unanimous 1971 decision of the Supreme Court requiring school boards to bus children where, as in the South, there was no other means of unifying school systems. While the exacerbated question of busing in northern de facto segregated districts was not covered in the Court's opinion, it was at least clear that the Court, despite its two new Nixon appointees, would not break with the tradition established by *Brown* v. *Topeka* in 1954. Again in 1971, when they allowed a busing order in Pontiac, Michigan, to stand, the judges exposed calculated political ambiguity.

The problem here is not at bottom a question of whether it is best to bus children from one school district to another or not to bus them. It is a problem, rather, of leadership. Robert Kennedy agreed with President Nixon that in some areas compulsory busing is unwise. As early as 1964, in his campaign for the Senate, Kennedy said, "compulsory transportation of children over long distances, away from the schools in their neighborhoods, doesn't make much sense and I am against it."[7]

But the whole force of his 1968 campaign for the Presidency was against any sort of ambivalence or equivocation. On the contrary, he made sure that the voters would know what to expect of him so that, should he win, there would be a majority for what he proposed to do. The elimination of de facto segregated education he believed to be bound up with the elimination of the ghetto itself. He frequently quoted black militant leader Floyd McKissick, who had said that "total reliance on integration—which amounts to reliance on acceptance by the white man—is at direct odds with that sense of control over one's destiny that . . . correlates so directly with achievement." The point was to "build communities of security and achievement and dignity. When that is done—when to carry a dark skin and come from Harlem or Hough is to say to the world, 'I share in a great enterprise in the life of this nation'—only then will America's promise of equality be fulfilled."[8] In the debate with McCarthy at the end of the California campaign he made the same point—integration by dispersal, like integration by busing, could not work until dispersal came through the ability of blacks to stand equal with whites.

Kennedy's position was unequivocal. It gave no comfort to white opponents of desegregation because it was so clearly directed at the causes of segregation. The leadership he proposed was not to delay desegregation but to push with all the powers of government, federal, state, and local, and all the force of private power that could be mustered toward rehabilitation of the inner cities and elimination of the poverty and deprivation which made of a black area not a neighborhood but a ghetto.

Because he proposed no program to achieve equality but only deplored violence and lawlessness, Richard Nixon could not win the trust of black voters. His plurality consisted largely, though not wholly, of whites united behind him not by hope or commitment to progressive change but by belief that he would put brakes on the changes that were in fact taking place. As President, Nixon was trapped by his own campaign posture. He could not lead the nation toward reconciliation of the races. His statement on segregation in the schools was an astute effort to give the appearance of leadership under conditions in which he could not in fact lead—since to lead, in these circumstances, meant to move, not to lag or to forestall movement.

On the other hand, Robert Kennedy, had he been elected, would have been free to provide leadership toward well-defined goals. Opposition would assuredly have been substantial. For example, analysis of his victory in the Indiana primary shows that white voters preferred McCarthy or Governor Roger Branigin by large margins. Kennedy carried black precincts by better than 90 percent while averaging no better than 35 percent in white precincts.[9] The same pattern held in California. Had he been elected in a contest with Nixon, as the Michigan Survey Research Center follow-up studies in 1969 indicated he would have done, he would, of course, have had white majorities in many areas. But he would as certainly have had very strong white opposition. His leadership—had he exercised it as he proposed to do—would have accented some national divisions as it had revealed them in the campaign.

The question, finally, is whether presidential leadership, made possible by the winning of a majority—however uneasy—behind a program, can survive and surmount the divisions that cannot be avoided if critical problems like racism and urban poverty are ever to be resolved. The continued validity of the presidential system would appear to depend on taking the risk. What is not, or should not be, in question is the certainty that presidential politics can at the best postpone (sometimes, of course, desirable in the short run) and at the worst may irretrievably exacerbate the crises it is intended to moderate and pacify.

It will no doubt be argued, cogently, that presidential politics may sometimes be salutary, even necessary, in the field of foreign policy. Surely there are occasions when it is important to disguise from other powers a President's true intent. The question is, *how* important? That question must be raised, no matter how caustically self-styled realists may object, because the risk of misleading Americans has to be weighed against the advantages of misleading others. There is also at least a possibility that the "others" will not in fact be fooled but that Americans will be. In the age of instant communication it is almost impossible to say different things to foreign and domestic audiences. The history of presidential politics in foreign policy reveals a nearly unbroken record of failure to greater or lesser degree. Polk's Oregon policy is sometimes offered as a successful instance of the politics of bluff. Secretary of State Buchanan himself at first thought it was bluff. But Polk's diary provides abundant evidence that the President was not bluffing, and that Buchanan, discovering this fact, was terrified lest Polk get the country into two wars at once. On any showing, failure of presidential politics in the foreign policy field is more serious than failure in attempts at leadership, since the President loses credibility both abroad and at home and thus diminishes his ability to govern.

Perhaps the most fateful, and instructive, instance of the consequences which may ensue from the substitution of presidential politics for presidential leadership is President

Johnson's conduct of United States relations with South Vietnam. It is not, of course, a question of whether Johnson's policy was correct but of how it was presented and defended over a period of years. In some respects the road from the Tonkin Resolution of 1964 to the conflagration of 1966 and after is similar to the road from Franklin Roosevelt's "quarantine the aggressor" speech of 1937, through the neutrality acts, the sale of arms to Britain and France, the destroyer-bases deal, the arming and convoying of merchant ships, to the declaration of war on December 8, 1941.

After his attempt at national leadership against fascism failed in 1937 for lack of popular support, Roosevelt advanced a policy of appearing to *avoid involvement* in order to justify steps of *increasing involvement*. A single instance is sufficiently illustrative. Shortly after the German invasion of Poland in September 1939, President Roosevelt asked Congress to amend the neutrality laws to permit belligerents to buy arms from the United States provided they transported the arms in their own ships. In the Congress and in the campaign of 1940 this measure was defended as a guarantee of noninvolvement because we gave up the right to carry military cargoes to belligerents. The fact, however, was that there was no way for Germany to take advantage of the policy, which was intended solely to favor England and France, and succeeded in doing so.[10] Roosevelt's reason for this sort of disingenuousness was that without American assistance the Western Allies would be defeated, with disastrous consequences for the United States. But since there was a great force of public opinion against any sort of involvement, American measures of support for the Allies could be revealed for what they were only as events unfolded; the cause of the Allies, ultimately England alone, deteriorated and the destructive terror of Nazism became evident. In retrospect Roosevelt's political skill appears to have served the nation well, and it can be argued that no other course would have succeeded. In any case, the Presidency itself was not demeaned and the majority of the public did not lose confidence in it or in Roosevelt. On the other hand, opponents of involvement had reasonable cause to complain that the issues were not candidly presented. Further, it is fair to say that national unity after December 7, 1941, was not owing to presidential politics but to the attack on the United States.

It would not be surprising if President Johnson, a disciple of Roosevelt, had the Roosevelt precedent in mind in the summer of 1964, when he was campaigning for the Presidency and searching for effective Vietnam policy at the same time. In any case it turned out to be a bad precedent. The Tonkin Resolution of August 1964 was understood in Congress as a sort of "blank check." But it was meant "for deposit only." The expectation was that the President would take measures to protect American ships operating in support of South Vietnam and to defend American support bases on the South Vietnamese mainland. Indeed, at the same moment Johnson was declaring that he would not send "American boys" to do what "Asian boys" should be doing. By the middle of 1965, however, the Resolution was regularly appealed to as authority for levying war against North Vietnam and the Viet Cong at any point in South Vietnam and for bombing the mainland of North Vietnam more intensively than the Allies had bombed Germany throughout the whole of World War II.

Unlike Roosevelt, President Johnson did not represent the measures which led to total involvement in Vietnam as means to avoid involvement. His stated objective was peace in a situation which could not, as he repeatedly asserted, be settled by war. What was disingenuous was the continuing effort to give the appearance that the expanding and escalating military measures were merely defensive, that the wholesale destruction of the enemy was for the purpose of securing a negotiated settlement.

In retrospect, it must be granted that the President did not go beyond the language of the Tonkin Resolution:

... the United States is, therefore, prepared, as the President determines, to take all necessary steps, including the use of armed force, to assist any member or protocol state of the Southeast Asia Collective Defense Treaty requesting assistance in defense of its freedom.[11]

On the basis of this wording it is not difficult to see why President Johnson and Secretary of State Rusk were constantly irritated by the argument, advanced later by senators and by leaders of the peace movement, that the United States was not obligated to assist South Vietnam under the Southeast Asia Treaty.

In 1964, however, the whole thrust of Johnson's campaign was to appear as the peace candidate. The Resolution seemed to be no more than a declaration by the whole United States that it would not be bullied or, better perhaps, would not be plagued by flies without swatting them. In this light it is useful to review some of the early steps toward overt involvement which followed the election.

In his foreign aid message to Congress in January 1965, Johnson asked for $500 million to "meet the frontal attack in Vietnam and Laos." But the next paragraph is more suggestive:

Indeed, $500 million may not be enough. I am therefore requesting for fiscal 1966 an additional stand-by authorization for military or supporting assistance which would be used only in Vietnam and only in case we should need more funds to protect our interests there.[12]

What such "interests" might be is not indicated. But that they were expanding in the President's mind was revealed a few weeks later in his historic speech at Johns Hopkins University:

Why must this nation hazard its ease and its interests and its power for the sake of a people so far away?

We fight because we must fight if we are to live in a world where every country can shape its own destiny. And only in such a world will our own freedom be finally secure.[13]

The language has the ring of a war message. Yet it was in the same speech that the President first said that he was "ready . . . for unconditional discussions" and offered to include North Vietnam in a development plan to which the United States would contribute a billion dollars.

A month later, in a special message to Congress asking for supplementary funds for use in Vietnam, the President spoke only of maintaining "the independence of South

Vietnam." At the same time he sought to bind the Congress to his policy by this unusual language:

For each member of Congress who supports this request is also voting to persist in our effort to halt Communist aggression in South Vietnam. Each is saying that the Congress and the President stand united before the world in joint determination that the independence of South Vietnam shall be preserved and Communist attack will not succeed.

In the same message, however, Johnson recognized the inadequacy, indeed, the tragic indecisiveness of military action:

For, in the long run, there can be no military solution to the problems of Vietnam. We must find the path to peaceful settlement. . . . We are still ready to talk, without conditions, to any government. We will go anywhere, discuss any subject, listen to any point of view in the interests of a peaceful solution.[14]

At this stage it became apparent to some senators and to others who were growing uneasy as step followed step toward deeper involvement that the President was identifying resistance to aggression with guaranteeing the independent sovereignty of South Vietnam. But since no such provision had been contained in the Geneva Accords of 1954 to which North Vietnam had agreed, it was hard to see what was meant by being ready to negotiate "without conditions."

By June the United States was sending combat as well as support troops. According to Secretary of Defense Robert McNamara, "the mission of our troops is to protect the bases on which we have very heavy concentrations of aircraft." However, the troops might be used in combat elsewhere, if the "Vietnamese lack the necessary reserves to effectively counter Viet Cong attacks."[15] The numbers of troops committed to Vietnam had risen from 20,000 in December 1964, just following the election, to about 75,000. At the end of July the numbers authorized reached 125,000. With each increase the President reiterated his policy of using only "carefully measured [steps] to do what must be done to bring an end to aggression and a peaceful settlement . . . a violent solution is impossible."[16]

It would be tedious to carry the narrative further. For more than two-and-one-half years thereafter the United

States escalated the war in the name of reaching a peaceful solution to an issue which the President insisted could not be resolved by military means. By March of 1968 there were well over half a million American soldiers in Vietnam, thousands of helicopters, combat aircraft, and warships. Hundreds of thousands of Vietnamese, North and South, and tens of thousands of Americans had been killed, and no end was in sight. President Johnson, united with an overwhelming majority of the people in 1964, was alienated from at least as many four years later. The failure of the war effort, accompanied often by official reports of success and prospects of success that turned out to be unrealized, led not only to loss of confidence in the President's ability to lead but in the integrity and the efficacy of the presidential system itself.*

That Lyndon Johnson, despite his unbroken confidence that he had been right, could put the integrity of his office into historic perspective, contrary to his own political interests, is the measure of his courage in retiring from the Presidency:

What we won when all of our people united just must not now be lost in suspicion and distrust and selfishness and politics among any of our people. And believing this as I do I have concluded that I should not permit the Presidency to become involved in the partisan divisions that are developing in this political year . . . .

Accordingly, I shall not seek, and I will not accept, the nomination of my party for another term as your President.[17]

It may be suggested that had Johnson's policy succeeded, as in a measure Roosevelt's had done, had Johnson, perhaps, been lucky, presidential politics would in retrospect look like presidential leadership. But Johnson's politics did not succeed, and on any showing it will not do to rest the case for the Presidency on a gamble for favorable turns of fortune. The consequences of failure, as in the case of John-

* It is a source of satisfaction, perhaps, but no comfort, that classified Pentagon documents revealed in June 1971 by various newspapers confirm the preceding analysis of President Johnson's rhetoric and underscore the grave implications here drawn from it.

son and Vietnam, may be unacceptable. President Nixon, nevertheless, presently undertook a similar gamble.

Not surprisingly, Richard Nixon's approach to the Vietnam problem in the campaign of 1968 was wholly political. In this respect his position was similar to all other candidates except, perhaps, Hubert Humphrey, who was bound by the circumstance of his office as Vice President to support the policy of the Johnson administration. But differences arise in a campaign on the extent to which politics is employed as means to election for its own sake or as means to election with a mandate to act according to proposals made to the voters. On the Vietnam issue in 1968 all candidates might be said to have asked for a mandate to end the war. But since this had always been the declared objective of the Johnson administration, and since there was no significant opposition to that objective, to declare oneself in favor of it, no matter how emphatically, could not be taken seriously as a proposal for the voters to reject or ratify.

Candidate Nixon's consistent strategy was to assert not only that he would end the war but that he had a plan for doing so. At the same time, by refusing, for persuasive reasons, to state what the plan was he avoided the kind of commitment to which, as President, he might be held. In the vernacular approved by both his immediate predecessors, he could "keep his options open." "Under no circumstances," he said at the outset of his campaign, "should a man say what he would do next January. The military situation may change, and we may have to take an entirely different tack."[18] He did not add that the voters in his own country could not, therefore, know what they were asked to vote for, even in general policy terms.

After President Johnson withdrew and negotiations at Paris commenced, Nixon joined the other candidates in a pledge not to speak on Vietnam in such a way as to jeopardize the peace talks. However, he was "for keeping pressure on militarily," and did not hesitate to criticize the administration's conduct of the war itself. Addressing the Republican Convention Resolutions Committee on August 1, he said, "until it [the war] is ended—and in order to hasten a negotiated end—it must be waged more effectively." He was not suggesting further escalation:

It requires a new strategy, which recognizes that this is a new and different kind of war. And it requires a fuller enlistment of our Vietnamese allies in their own defense . . . .

The Administration had done far too little, too late to train and equip the South Vietnamese, both for fighting their own war now and for the task of defending their own country after the war is settled . . . .

. . . the old style conventional military aspects have been over-emphasized and [the war's] other dimensions—psychological, political, economic, even diplomatic, have gotten too little attention.

Again he declined to make specific suggestions: "Anything he [the Republican nominee] might offer as a candidate would become unavailable for bargaining when he became President." Finally, he held out the promise that if the war were still going on in January 1969, it could best be ended "by a new Administration that has given no hostages to the mistakes of the past; an Administration neither defending old errors nor bound by the old record."[19]

If, as President, Nixon was not responsible for the Johnson policy or record, he was in unmeasured debt to its achievement. When his own plan was revealed, it turned out to be wholly dependent upon the state of military affairs won by the massive American intervention—and to be hardly a "plan" at all, but only the next phase in the continuity of Johnson's policy. In the summer of 1969 he began to withdraw combat troops, announcing that South Vietnamese were being trained to take their place. His policy was to de-escalate the war by "Vietnamizing" it. At the same time, Vietnamizing was defined as ending the war. In a full-length address in November he told of "new orders."

Under the new orders, the primary mission of our troops is to enable the South Vietnamese forces to assume the full responsibility for the security of South Vietnam . . . .

And now we have begun to see the results of this long overdue change in American policy in Vietnam . . . . After five years of Americans going into Vietnam we are finally bringing American men home.[20]

What he did not say was that the men were coming home because they had been going over. The "new orders" were precisely those which had sent advisers to Vietnam under Eisenhower and John Kennedy and massive combat forces under Johnson. It would be gratuitous to observe that Johnson himself would have brought home troops in proportion as they were no longer needed.

What was different in the Nixon formulation was the language in which it was expressed. Taking over at the point when established policy would in any case call for systematic withdrawal of troops, President Nixon sought to give the appearance of promulgating new policy "to end the war."

> Let me now turn to our program for the future. We have adopted a plan which we have worked out in cooperation with the South Vietnamese for the complete withdrawal of all United States combat ground forces and their replacement by South Vietnamese on an orderly scheduled timetable.
>
> This withdrawal will be made from strength and not from weakness. As South Vietnamese become stronger, the rate of American withdrawal can become greater.

That this was not in fact a plan for "ending the war" but a policy of continuing it was implicit. But the President presently made it nearly explicit: "If I conclude that increased enemy action jeopardizes our remaining forces in Vietnam, I shall not hesitate to take strong and effective measures to deal with that situation." Forces other than ground combat troops would thus remain in Vietnam indefinitely. If the combination of Vietnamese ground troops, American air and support forces, plus whatever other "allied" troops and matériel were available proved insufficient to continue the momentum then achieved, Nixon would "take strong and effective measures."

Like Johnson, however, President Nixon saw "only two choices" to end the war. "Precipitate withdrawal" would be defeat and unacceptable, and would cause "our allies" to "lose confidence in America," and we "would lose confidence in ourselves." The other choice, to continue the war in order to end it, was cast in the same form as Johnson had cast it: "search for a just peace through a negotiated settlement." Nixon, however, went on to recognize that such a settlement might well depend on "continued implementation of our plan for Vietnamization." In short, there was real prospect of a very long war.

Knowing well enough that some critics would draw their conclusions from what was implicit rather than his explicit statements, the President paid his respects to the dissenters:

> In San Francisco a few weeks ago, I saw demonstrators carrying signs reading, "Lose in Vietnam. Bring the boys home."
> Well, one of the strengths of our free society is that any American has a right to reach that conclusion and to adopt that point of view.
> But as President of the United States, I would be untrue to my oath of office to be dictated to by the minority . . . .

Like Johnson, he put the matter in terms of polar opposites. Either win or lose. The appeal ultimately was to patriotism:

> So tonight, to you, the great silent majority of my fellow Americans, I ask for your support. I pledged in my campaign for the Presidency to end the war in a way that we could win the peace.
> I have initiated a plan of action which will enable me to keep that pledge. The more support I can have from the American people, the sooner that pledge can be redeemed. For the more divided we are at home, the less likely the enemy is to negotiate in Paris.
> Let us be united for peace. Let us also be united against defeat. Because let us understand: North Vietnam cannot defeat or humiliate the United States. Only Americans can do that.

How prolonging the war was going to end it; how the peace was to be won without winning the war militarily; how Hanoi was to agree to negotiate because the United States was "ending the war" were questions which, in the immediate aftermath of the speech, seemed not to trouble a substantial majority. The President's ratings in the polls went up and, in particular, his conduct of the war was approved.

For months thereafter, the popular yearning for an end to the war seemed to find expression in the President. Troops were in fact coming home, and national concern seemed to be abating. Unlike his unfortunate predecessor,

Nixon had apparently found a political formulation which obviated or, at least, delayed the imperative of presidential leadership. By April 1970, despite the overthrow of Prince Sihanouk, and increasing North Vietnamese and Viet Cong activity in Cambodia, the "Vietnamization" program appeared to have won massive popular support at home and some lessening of criticism abroad. In a major address the President, scotching rumors that he would be forced by military circumstances to slow down the withdrawal of troops, announced that he would bring home 150,000 more within a year. This would mean continued withdrawals at the rate already established, though the command in the field was allowed a considerable measure of flexibility.

The speech itself was consummately political. While Nixon acknowledged "with regret that no progress has taken place on the negotiating front," he found it nevertheless possible to assert that "we finally have in sight the just peace we are seeking."[21] At the same time, he solemnly warned the other side: "If I conclude that increased enemy action jeopardizes our remaining forces in Vietnam, I shall not hesitate to take strong and effective measures to deal with that situation." As for the "just peace" that was said to be in sight, it would be "a political solution that reflects the will of the South Vietnamese people to determine their future without outside interference." However, "a fair political solution should reflect the existing relationship of forces within South Vietnam." And he recognized "the complexity of shaping machinery that would fairly apportion political power in South Vietnam. We are flexible; we have offered nothing on a take-it-or-leave-it basis."[22]

Again, the organizing principle was ambiguity: peace was in sight though no progress toward it had been made; troops would continue to be withdrawn but the war might be escalated; the peace would secure self-determination for South Vietnam, but would reflect the military situation. Yet the force of the speech was to suggest that the new policy of the new administration was getting results—the boys were coming home and the war would be over within a reasonable time.

Precisely because the President was employing a politics of paradox, his decision, only ten days later, to extend the war to Cambodia was at once shocking and predictable. It was less understandable that he would leave himself open to a charge of deception by allowing Secretary of State William Rogers to withhold information from the Senate Foreign Relations Committee even after the decision had been made. But the rhetoric of his address announcing the decision was cut to the familiar pattern.[23] He reminded the nation and the world that he had warned the Communist forces that he would "take strong and effective measures" if they increased their pressures and threatened the lives of Americans. Now, he said, they have done precisely that. At the same time, he recalled that Communist bases in Cambodia had been in full operation for five years, threatening the security of South Vietnam and the lives of Americans fighting there. We did not move "against those sanctuaries because we did not wish to violate the territory of a neutral nation." Now, however, the Communist troops were moving on Phnom Penh, and Cambodia had asked for assistance. Somehow the presumed threat to the Cambodian capital was a greater threat than had been the five years of attacks on South Vietnamese and Americans on the Vietnam side of the line. "If this Communist effort succeeds, Cambodia would become a vast enemy staging area and springboard for attacks on South Vietnam." It would also be a "refuge where enemy troops could return from combat without fear of retaliation." In short, one could not avoid observing, the President was accusing the Communists of doing what they were doing, and had been doing for five years. What was in fact new, of course, was the coup against Sihanouk and the announced intent of the Communists, including the Russians and the Chinese, to restore him to power. But the President said nothing of Sihanouk. He spoke only of "the government of Cambodia."

The President set forth three possible courses of action: 1) to do nothing, which would "gravely endanger" the Americans remaining in Vietnam after the next withdrawal; 2) give massive assistance to Cambodia—impractical because the Cambodian army "could not rapidly and effectively use it"; 3) "go to the heart of the trouble. That means cleaning out major North Vietnamese and Viet Cong occupied sanctuaries which serve as bases for attacks on both Cambodia and American and South Vietnamese forces in South Vietnam." A fair translation might be, "we have decided to do now what some advisers, military and civilian, have been urging for five years—extend the war into Cambodia in order to destroy the Communist forces we have not been able to destroy in South Vietnam or by bombing North Vietnam, and thus win the war."

The operation, President Nixon asserted, was "not an invasion of Cambodia." This was so for the remarkable reason that "the areas in which these attacks will be launched are completely occupied and controlled by North Vietnamese forces." The logic of this view was apparently lost on the Cambodian foreign minister who lodged a quiet but formal protest against unauthorized incursions on Cambodian territory by South Vietnamese and American soldiers. The protest was not pressed, of course, since the government of Cambodia now had reason to hope that it would be secured by American power.

The purpose of the whole endeavor, the President continued, was to satisfy the wishes of the "majority of the American people": to withdraw American troops from Vietnam, to end the war, and to keep down the casualties. Had the President not made this decision "the credibility of the United States would be destroyed in every area of the world where only the power of the United States deters aggression." At this point his adherence to the policy of his predecessor was explicit. Lyndon Johnson had said the same thing a hundred times to explain his belief that only by escalation could de-escalation and peace be achieved.

Like Johnson, President Nixon sought to persuade "the leaders of North Vietnam . . . that we will be patient in working for peace, we will be conciliatory at the conference table, but we will not be humiliated." In the same breath there was an echo of Douglas MacArthur arguing with President Truman on the strategy of the Korean War almost twenty years earlier: "We will not allow American men by the thousands to be killed by an enemy from privileged sanctuaries."

Toward the end of his speech Nixon mounted to the level of grand strategy to meet the world crisis:

We live in an age of anarchy both abroad and at home. We see mindless attacks on all the great institutions which have been created by free civilizations in the last five hundred years. Here in the United States, great universities are being systematically destroyed. Small nations all over the world find themselves under attack from within and from without.

If when the chips are down the U.S. acts like a pitiful helpless giant, the forces of totalitarianism and anarchy will threaten free nations and free institutions throughout the world.

The President, who had pronounced at Guam the "Nixon Doctrine" that troubled nations would thereafter have to do their own fighting, now seemed to be saying that they must be able to depend on the United States.

It is not our power but our will and character that is being tested. The question all Americans must ask and answer is this: Does the richest and strongest nation in the history of the world have the character to meet a direct challenge by a group which rejects every effort to win a just peace, ignores our warning, tramples on solemn agreements, violates the neutrality of an unarmed people, and uses our prisoners as hostages?

If we failed to meet this challenge all other nations will be on notice that despite its overwhelming power the United States, when a real crisis comes, will be found wanting.

In the end he turned to the politics of his own position and rested his decision and his plea for support on the calculated ambiguity of his campaign in 1968:

My fellow Americans: During my campaign for the Presidency, I pledged to bring Americans home from Vietnam. They are coming home.

I promised to end the war. I shall keep that promise.

I promised to win a just peace. I shall keep that promise.

But we are also determined to put an end to this war.

Invoking memories of Wilson, Franklin Roosevelt, Eisenhower, and John Kennedy, Nixon concluded by defying his opponents. He was prepared to risk the loss of Republican seats in the congressional election and his own defeat in 1972:

> ... I have rejected all political considerations in making this decision . . . .
>
> I would rather be a one-term President than be a two-term President at the cost of seeing America become a second-rate power and see this nation accept the first defeat in its proud 190 year history.

Whatever might be the political consequences of this political rejection of politics, one historic consequence was that it could not enhance the prestige and effectiveness of the Presidency by leading a majority toward the achievement of defined and agreed upon goals. At best, it could persuade a majority for a time to trust the President; at worst, it could greatly diminish his ability to govern in the realm of foreign policy. The opinion polls once more revealed the potency of presidential rhetoric. A majority was prepared, for a time, to trust Mr. Nixon. Before the President sent troops into Cambodia some 70 percent were reported by the Harris Survey to be opposed to such a course. A few days after he had done so, the Gallup Poll found that 51 percent approved while 35 percent disapproved and 14 percent were uncertain.

But such sudden reversals of opinion on Vietnam tactics had often occurred before. At each major escalation during the Johnson administration a majority had temporarily been rallied behind the President. The prospect that one more push, one more new angle of attack, would somehow bring an end to the war and to the frustration of the country renewed hope. Indeed, what was remarkable about Nixon's Cambodia speech was that the majority it rallied was so small, while the fury of the opposition was unprecedented.

The President's critics, led by a nearly unanimous Senate Foreign Relations Committee, asked questions which cut through the politics of his statement to the core of his action: how could lives be saved by sending more men into new battles? how could the war be ended by extending it into another country? how could invasion not be invasion? how could patience for negotiation be displayed by opening new fronts in the war? how could confidence in the Presidency be maintained when the President deliberately provoked a question of constitutional authority? how could credibility be buttressed by duplicity? That such questions at such a perilous moment could be raised by men in responsible posts of government under the Constitution revealed a crisis in the presidential system and underscored the risks of preferring presidential politics to presidential leadership.

The Cambodian decision, followed as it was six months later by renewed bombing of "selected targets" in the North, focused attention once more on the question of presidential power. With the coming of weapons of total destruction and their intercontinental ballistic carriers, the authority of the American President has reached out to every corner of the world. When nuclear conflagration could be a matter of minutes, trust in the President becomes a matter of overriding consequence. Declarations of war by the Congress, indeed, any significant participation by the Congress in vital decision-making becomes a problem of a different sort from any known before. As President Johnson escalated the Vietnam war, many senators had questioned not only his policy but his authority. And in the campaign of 1968 Senator McCarthy had raised the larger question of limiting the powers of the President. In the wake of President Nixon's Cambodia decision the Senate sought ways to place a time limit upon American action in that country, refused funds for combat forces not only in Cambodia but in Thailand and Laos as well, and reopened the whole question of using the congressional power of the purse to end the war. Thus the President was forced to defend not only his policy but his office.

It would be as tedious as it is unnecessary to make a similar analysis of the rhetoric in which the Laos invasion of 1971 was reported and discussed by the President. The only important differences were that American support was confined to advice and to massive air firepower, since ground-troop participation was prohibited by law, and that the South Vietnamese forces were driven back with little if any significant success. Again, the action was described as a tactic to end the war, to bring home the American troops, and to secure a just and honorable peace. Again, the war was in fact widened, large areas were laid waste and more thousands of noncombatants became refugees. American troops continued to come home. But there was no sign of peace in any part of Indo-China. And the American presence was everywhere, if not in manpower, in firepower and in the economic support without which no one maintained that the South Vietnamese government could survive. The cost at home was a still deeper cleavage between the President and the Congress, as the crisis of leadership continued.

It would be rash to suggest that the presidential crisis of the 1970s was wholly owing to the failure of the campaign of 1968. But it would be foolish not to see that failures in that campaign contributed to failures in presidential leadership afterwards. The Vietnam issue was only the most immediately pressing of the many which were never seriously debated after Robert Kennedy's death. Had he lived, win or lose, the conception of the role of the President which dictated his mode of campaigning would at the least have forced other candidates either to state proposals, or to agree with his, or to reveal an incapacity for leadership. The public would have been led to consider the war issue in something other than the simplistic terms of "withdraw now," or "I can end the war sooner than he can," or "I have a plan" but will not tell you what it is. At the best, unlikely perhaps but abundantly worth the effort, a President could have been elected by a majority persuaded that his proposals for dealing with the problem were best and deserved to be tried under his leadership. Democracy is no guarantee of the correctness or, certainly, the good fortune of policies approved by the voters. But even failure is better for the Republic when it is understood and shared by a majority that has won an election over a freely dissenting minority in a clearly articulated campaign. The risk that the Republic will be torn apart by bitter, even irreconcilable divisions, is greatly diminished.

Because of her good fortune in resources, geography, literacy, and inheritance of the rule of law, as well as other characteristics which have distinguished her from other countries, the United States has had only episodic experience with sharply defined issues in sharply fought presidential elections. For the same reasons American political parties have normally been organized for the purpose of selecting candidates and winning elections rather than winning support for specific programs and policies. More often than not the parties have functioned to gloss over divisions and distinctions in order to appeal as nearly as possible to everybody. The result is to place excessive emphasis on the personalities of presidential candidates, to exaggerate immediate and evanescent issues out of all proportion to their real importance, to touch great issues gingerly and rhetorically, and to leave the ultimate sovereign question of responsibility undefined. When winning for its own sake is the highest priority of the parties, candidates are almost irresistibly tempted to avoid the commitments of leadership by the practice of presidential politics. This is what happened in 1968, and what Robert Kennedy's campaign sought to forestall.

The Kennedy campaign itself was representative of a counter tradition in American presidential politics which has, on occasion, produced leaders of uncommon courage and talent, with quite different consequences for the Republic. The Presidency, in fact, has survived for some two centuries not because many Presidents have been content to use, or not use, their powers to maintain a comfortable status quo, as their supporters perhaps wished them to do, but because some Presidents have been first-rate practitioners of the politics of presidential leadership. If the presidential system is to survive the strains and crises of the present era, that kind of leadership, as Kennedy so strongly urged, will have to be revived.

SIX

The Politics of Presidential Leadership:
Parties, Candidates, and the President

Because American political parties are concerned primarily with generating majorities, not mandates, a presidential candidate who seeks a mandate must work to shape his party as an indispensable instrument of his success in winning and, after winning, doing, as Franklin Roosevelt's 1936 campaign illustrates. Unhappily, the overweening preoccupation of American politicians with winning has tended more and more to militate against seeking a mandate at all. The parties will not or cannot shape themselves, nor will their congressional leadership. An historic experiment made by the Democrats in 1957, after Adlai Stevenson's second defeat by President Eisenhower, reveals some of the dimensions of the problem.

Governor Stevenson, in the campaign of 1952, had brought an invigorating flow of young people into the Democratic party and even charged a good many veterans with a new excitement. It was not only his attractiveness as a person and an orator that confirmed the leadership he was drafted to undertake but his remarkably articulate concern for ideas and programs, and his belief that the overriding purpose of presidential campaigns was not so much winning as taking "advantage of this great quadrennial opportunity to debate issues sensibly and soberly."[1] "A man," he said, overoptimistically no doubt, "doesn't save a century, or a civilization, but a militant party wedded to a principle can."[2] For the four years following, Stevenson was accepted generally throughout his party and the country (except, perhaps, in the South)—indeed throughout the world—as the authentic spokesman of the American opposition. He spoke and wrote often and authoritatively. On great domestic issues like McCarthyism, and in all important questions of foreign policy, he was careful to consult Speaker Sam Rayburn and Senate Majority Leader Lyndon Johnson, as well as other party leaders. Ideas and suggestions for speeches flowed in to him from many sources. One of these, a group which met frequently at the New York home of Thomas K. Finletter, was a sort of "shadow cabinet," in the British manner. Stevenson himself was something like a shadow President.

After Stevenson's defeat in 1952 it had been generally assumed that he would be nominated again, but when, in November 1956, after his second defeat, he formally withdrew from further presidential competition, there was no obvious successor. To fill the vacuum of leadership thus created, Stevenson proposed that the national chairman, Paul Butler, appoint an advisory council as an arm of the Democratic National Committee with responsibility for criticizing the government as a loyal opposition, and developing positions alternative to those of the administration.

Butler, with the consent of the National Committee, established the Democratic Advisory Council with Stevenson, former President Truman, Governor Averell Harriman of New York, Governor Mennen Williams of Michigan, and several National Committeemen as a nucleus of membership. Speaker Rayburn and Majority Leader Johnson were invited to represent the Democratic Congress. But after careful, if brief, consideration the congressional leadership rejected the invitation and sought to downgrade the Advisory Council by asserting that the leadership of the party in fact rested with them. Senators Estes Kefauver, defeated candidate for Vice President, and Stuart Symington, Hubert Humphrey, and John F. Kennedy, as potential presidential candidates, were invited to join the council and did so. But during the council's four-year life it functioned without direct liaison and little informal coordination with the congressional leadership.

Partly because of Stevenson's personal stature and partly because all the likely presidential candidates for 1960, except Johnson, were members, the Advisory Council succeeded in its mission to a remarkable degree. Sustained by donations from many of Stevenson's friends, from political supporters of one or another of the candidates, and from many people who were hopeful that it might shape the Democratic party into a more effective instrument of government, the Advisory Council set up task forces on such subjects as foreign policy, defense, peace and disarmament, science, agriculture, the economy, and civil rights. These subcommittees drew upon the resources of universities, private research agencies, and, of course, Democratic politicians to produce a remarkable series of position papers which, in turn, were debated, revised, and published by the Advisory Council itself as official pronouncements of the Democratic party. Stevenson and the presidential hopefuls made abundant use of the council's work in their speeches and writings throughout the second Eisenhower administration.

Perhaps the ultimate proof of the council's value was its contribution to the campaign of 1960. Senator Kennedy, familiar from the start with the council's deliberations and papers, based his campaign largely upon them and, to an extent, drew for campaign and postelection preparatory staff directly upon the talent the council had recruited. Thus such central elements of the Kennedy campaign and presidential program as the "new economics" of Walter Heller and others, the Arms Control and Disarmament Agency, the use of executive power to make progress in the field of civil rights despite a dilatory Congress, and the Alliance for Progress had important sources in the Democratic Advisory Council.

But the very effectiveness of the Advisory Council in generating and articulating policy and program ironically underscored the weakness of the party system and candidate Kennedy's inability to unite and lead the Democrats. As usual, many congressional candidates in 1960 separated themselves almost entirely from the presidential race—especially in the South—and most were cautious in their endorsements of Kennedy proposals lest they offend some significant group of voters in their constituencies. Thus Kennedy, as candidate, was forced to campaign for popular support of a program without the organized support of his own party and, in some places, even against it. As President, it followed, Kennedy could only carry out his campaign pledges by overcoming the resistance of many members of his own party in Congress.

Since his election was by so narrow a margin that he could not face the Congress with a mandate, it is not remarkable that he was forced to move slowly. What is remarkable is that he accomplished as much as he did. As his personal prestige rose, his political value to congressmen facing the election of 1962 rose with it. And there is no doubt that Kennedy's leadership brought the executive and congressional wings of his party much closer together in that election and thereby greatly increased the prospects of enactment of his program. Had the forces of the party marshalled in the Democratic Advisory Council been joined cooperatively with the Democratic forces in Congress in 1957, if necessary without most of the Southern members, it is probable that Kennedy would have won by a significantly larger margin in 1960, and achievement of his campaign proposals would not have had to await the next election and the national trauma of his assassination.

Rarely does a presidential candidate combine qualities of inspiring leadership with both a positive program and political good fortune. In this century only Theodore Roosevelt (in 1904), Woodrow Wilson, Franklin Roosevelt, and Lyndon Johnson had been wholly successful as candidates. Wilson, a masterful orator, had been a student of democratic governments for years. In his studies of cabinet and congressional government in the United States he had displayed and deplored the weakness of the executive under "whig" presidents, and had compared the American system unfavorably with the British. As a candidate in 1912 he sought to unite the Democratic party under his personal leadership behind a promise of reforms that combined some of the features of the Republican-led progressive movement with the populism of William Jennings Bryan, to whom he owed his nomination. It was Wilson's good fortune that the opposition was hopelessly divided. But the well-articulated program of the Progressives, dramatically led by Theodore Roosevelt, and the more conservative but equally well articulated defense of the administration by President Taft provided the nation with a competition of proposals as well as candidates in which the winner could claim a mandate. Wilson won a massive electoral victory, a substantial plurality among the three candidates, and led his party to an immense congressional victory. If the results were to an extent fortuitous, the consequences were implicit in the campaign itself. And the historic achievements of Wilson's first term were impressive testimony to the putting into practice of his theory of the strong Presidency.

The most overwhelming presidential victories of this century were scored by Franklin Roosevelt in 1936 and Lyndon Johnson in 1964. In these somewhat similar campaigns there were no important third parties (despite some right-wing cacophony in 1936) to complicate the issues or divide the vote. Roosevelt, defending the social and economic experimentation of his first term, promised to continue. He asked specifically for a vote of confidence in the social security program, the great thrust toward public power development, and the new charter of organized labor. Governor Alfred Landon, on behalf of the Republicans, accepted the challenge and vigorously debated the record and the issues, sometimes, as he afterwards candidly confessed, against his own better judgement. The result was such a massive Democratic majority that for the next two years, except on the Supreme Court issue, Roosevelt could count on a majority in both houses composed entirely of pro-Roosevelt Democrats from above the Mason-Dixon line. The Fair Labor Standards Act is probably the most enduring as it was the most radical measure of Roosevelt's strong Presidency so unmistakably confirmed at the polls.[3]

President Johnson's campaign of 1964 was at least as devoted to issues, and his leadership was also emphatically confirmed by the voters. However much of his success was dependent on the mantle he had inherited from John F.

Kennedy—and he felt a deep obligation to work for the Kennedy program—there was no doubt that he would continue the fight for equal rights, promote and strengthen the "new economics," and give new emphasis to the war on poverty. His victory, like Roosevelt's in 1936, gave him a mandate to continue, with a firm congressional majority of northern and western democrats responsive to his leadership. It was paradoxical but understandable that Senator Goldwater's strength was in the "democratic" South, where he carried five states.

Harry Truman's unhappy experience after his victory in 1948 is less an example of defective presidential leadership than of an inherent weakness of the party system. Despite his attractive and persistent campaigning for practical steps toward racial equality, a national health program, and a national effort to renew the cities, Truman was never able to put his program through the Congress; indeed, he was more than once faced with the necessity of vetoing major legislation enacted directly contrary to his recommendations. Only in foreign affairs, where the issues were less divisive and he received decisive help from some Republicans, was he able to exert the leadership he believed a President should give.

Truman's failure was a predictable outcome of the Democratic convention which nominated him. In the preceding months many liberals and some party organization leaders had talked of dumping the President as a likely loser. Had not General Eisenhower flatly refused to run he might have been nominated at the Democratic convention.

With the Eisenhower balloon pricked, Truman's difficulties were nevertheless enormous. There was a left-of-center split led by former Vice President Henry Wallace, who attracted some liberal leaders and left-wing unions to his candidacy on a Progressive party ticket calling for an end to the cold war. On the conservative side there was a determined anti-Truman movement in the South. At issue was civil rights. On the convention floor a group of "young Turks," led by Mayor Hubert Humphrey of Minneapolis, and future governors Mennen Williams of Michigan and

Adlai E. Stevenson of Illinois, succeeded in defeating the empty compromise plank the Southern delegates had reluctantly accepted, and won instead adoption of a strong plank specifically endorsing a fair employment practices law. At the climax of the fight, the first staged before a national television audience, many Southern delegates walked out. Only days later, a States-Rights Democratic ("Dixiecrat") party was launched, with Governor Strom Thurmond of South Carolina as candidate for President. Truman, for his part, accepted the nomination and the civil rights platform with enthusiasm.

The three-way split of the Democratic party placed Truman at an initial disadvantage which for a long time seemed insuperable. The election results were a personal tribute to the President, but as the convention and the campaign foreshadowed, his victory was scored to an important extent in spite of his party, not because of it. While he defeated Republican Thomas E. Dewey by better than two million votes, his margin was somewhat less than half the total votes cast. The Democrats won the House by ninety-two seats, but a large minority were openly or quietly sympathetic to the Dixiecrat movement and opposed to the President on many issues. The margin in the Senate, twelve seats, was even less impressive since it was more dependent on anti-civil rights Southern members than was the House majority. Thus President Truman returned to the White House with no usable mandate. Convinced of the necessity for a strong Presidency and fully prepared to exercise all the power he could summon, he was nevertheless usually frustrated in his efforts to do what he thought needed to be done. He was clearly a victim not of defects in the presidential system as such, but of the irresponsible pluralism of the parties.

Harry Truman's second term was marred to an extent by his own lack of judgment in backing venal subordinates who were his long-time friends—a defect of the virtue of loyalty. But, on the larger scale, it was not headline grabbing corruption so much as his inability to lead his party that accounted for his failures in domestic policy. The case of his successor was even sorrier in this regard. Eisenhower, winning twice by immense margins, was never able to exert effective leadership over the Republican party, and most often did not try. In his campaigns he relied almost exclusively on his personal popularity, avoiding even the discussion of the more divisive issues and proposing no programs to meet the ever more imperious demands of decaying cities, the widening poverty gap, and racial tension. Stevenson, his defeated opponent, sought to persuade his party to work for a program of specific measures, but had only a limited success and could not, in any case, hope to match Eisenhower's magic hold on the affection of the country. It is worth noting, however, that Stevenson's efforts in 1956 to establish a position on civil rights acceptable to at least some Southerners not only prevented a walkout at the Democratic convention of that year but contributed greatly to Senate Majority Leader Lyndon Johnson's success in passing the first civil rights law since Reconstruction. The margin in the Senate on that bill was provided by four Southern supporters of Stevenson plus Johnson himself.

It is not surprising that political parties long habituated to avoiding divisive issues should tend either to disintegrate or to fall victim to paralysis of the will. Both tendencies are discernible in the Democratic and Republican parties today. But there is another equally disheartening cause of the decline in party prestige and effectiveness. Parties which seek to include everybody, as Adlai Stevenson once observed, may end by pleasing nobody. If it is normal for American parties to reflect the pluralism of American society, so it is normal for the parties to become more plural and divided with the increasing diversity and complexity of the problems the society evolves, or simply allows to happen. But the more plural a party is, the less it is able to discipline itself and the less likely it is to be a viable instrument either of government or of opposition. Under such conditions a temporary political party or faction formed around a single issue can seriously diminish the strength of the regular organization. Thus the McCarthy campaign of 1968, concentrating on peace, split off liberals as well as some conservatives from each of the parties, while the Wallace candidacy, concentrating on "law and order" with segregationist overtones, wholly destroyed the effectiveness of the Democratic party in the South. In the showdown neither Nixon nor Humphrey could exert more than formal leadership over his party.

In the aftermath Humphrey, as titular leader of the Democratic party, seemed for a time almost to disappear as an important opposition leader. While such other Democrats as Senators Mike Mansfield, Edmund Muskie, George McGovern, and Edward Kennedy could speak collectively with an effective voice on some issues, they had no real hope of re-forming the old Roosevelt-Truman-Stevenson or even the newer Johnson-Kennedy coalition save, perhaps, as a negative reaction to President Nixon. Senator McCarthy, having led a campaign against the Democratic organization and having denounced it at the 1968 convention, had little leverage with which to propel himself toward party leadership. For reasons best known to himself he made no effort to use what support he had developed for that purpose. As President, Richard Nixon chose to use the patronage not to build the Republican party so much as to work toward his own reelection by a class and regional alignment of forces trusting him to reduce crime and to block or at least to moderate the pace of social change.

Robert Kennedy was a party man, a loyal Democrat. Unlike Senator McCarthy, he stated flatly at the outset of his campaign that he would support the Democratic nominee regardless of which candidate was the winner. But the whole thrust of his encouragement of the "new politics" was the effort to shape the Democratic party into an instrument for radical but controlled and disciplined change. Toward the end of the California campaign he spoke at some length about the "politics of citizen participation."

Of course Americans have always participated in their political life, and worked in political campaigns. What is different about 1968 is the extent and quality of that work. People—students and teachers, housewives and professionals—have worked not just in the primary states, but in precinct caucuses and county conventions; seeking not to serve the candidate selected by the party machinery, but to exercise democratic choice. Beyond this, they have engaged hundreds of thousands, perhaps millions, of their fellow-citizens in a face-to-face discussion and debate, not just about the merits of one or another candidate, but about the substantive issues which are at the heart of the election.[4]

The "new politics" of 1968, Kennedy said, must mean "an end to some of the clichés and stereotypes of past political rhetoric." His own campaign was short on such rhetoric and long on discussion of issues and advocacy of programs and policies. Had he been elected he would have been obligated, and mandated as were the Roosevelts or Lyndon Johnson, to continue the effort. He would have had to work to reform the Democratic party as a central element in the complex of forces he needed to manage and direct in order to move toward the realization of the goals he sought. Whether he would have succeeded is, again, wholly speculative. But what is not speculative is that both parties continued to founder after 1968 for lack of the sort of leadership he proposed, and are likely to continue to do so until they get it.

In some matters, however, President Nixon sought to exert leadership for the enactment of positive programs. An important instance is welfare reform. His message to Congress on welfare in August 1969 was remarkable on several counts, not the least of which was its unexpectedness. The plan called for a modest "guaranteed annual income" of $1600 for a family of four, uniform throughout the fifty states. There would be employment incentive through a formula allowing working heads of families to retain their welfare payments on a diminishing scale up to the point where they earned $3,920 a year or slightly above the official "poverty line." A recipient would be required to take a job if one were offered or forfeit his assistance allowance. The old regulation that forbade assistance to a family so long as the father was earning any money at all would be eliminated.[5] None of these provisions had been proposed in

Nixon's campaign for President, and some had been categorically opposed. It is not surprising, under such circumstances, that his chief critics were in his own party and that he had to place unusually heavy reliance on Democratic congressional leadership to guide the program into law. The point is not, of course, to quarrel with a good law because it comes into being by unexpected means, but to regret the failure of the election campaign to provide the people with real choices and a justified sense of participation in the making of great decisions.

In the early stages of the 1968 campaign Nixon spoke scarcely at all of welfare except to repeat what no one disputed, namely, that the current system was unsatisfactory. In May he announced that he was trying to devise a substitute for public welfare because the system had a "demeaning effect" on many recipients.[6] If it was not reassuring that a presidential candidate felt compelled to say that he "could not now specify how to accomplish" his purpose, it was at least refreshingly candid. More than two months later, however, he had made little progress. At a national meeting of county commissioners in Washington, attended also by Humphrey and Wallace, Nixon announced that he was opposed to a "guaranteed income" or a "negative income tax." He proposed instead "vast compensatory education" for the poor and a program of job training in private industry.[7] Since such programs were already in effect and unopposed by the other candidates, Nixon had apparently not yet decided to take a leadership position on the issue. Nor had he by the end of September, when the campaign was at its height. Opposing the idea of a guaranteed income once more, he played on the words of John F. Kennedy: "What made this country great," said Nixon, "is not what the government did for the people but what the people did for themselves."[8] Only at the last moment did he speak of a new approach to welfare. Calling for a "national standard" that would reduce disparities in welfare payments among the states, he declared, "we ought to provide an adequate standard of welfare . . . we ought to recognize that this is one country.''[9] But he still offered no suggestions as to how he would propose to do it.

If in the end Nixon's campaign did provide a clue as to what he might propose as President a year later, one can hardly accept a guessing game as an effort of leadership to educate the people and persuade a majority to support a great national policy. And there was, in the aftermath, a degree of irony in President Nixon's choice of Daniel Patrick Moynihan, a leading Democratic brain truster and a supporter of Robert Kennedy, as his chief adviser on urban affairs. It was Moynihan who devised the Nixon welfare plan and helped to persuade the President to reverse himself on the principle of a guaranteed minimum annual income.

That Nixon did not propose his welfare program during the election campaign is especially regrettable because it was not only a progressive measure calling for presidential leadership but politically attractive and viable. The idea of a minimum allowance for all the poor could reassure many disheartened and alienated people. The incentive to work while still receiving assistance could raise justifiable hopes that poverty might eventually be overcome. The plan even carried some hope that the animosity of white poor toward black poor in and near the ghettoes could be mitigated. Conservative Republicans would have resisted and this, no doubt, was one reason the candidate persisted in his negative attitude. Yet because the poorer states, especially in the South, would benefit by much higher standards of welfare assistance at relatively much less cost to their taxpayers, even Nixon's "southern strategy" would have been advanced. With its intrinsic merit and its political appeal the Nixon plan, had it been proposed in the campaign, would have forced Humphrey to sharpen his own more traditional proposals. The nation as a whole, not simply the poor, would have gained a better understanding of the problem and possible approaches to its resolution. Had Robert Kennedy lived to contest the election it is safe to guess that he would have challenged Nixon to say where the jobs were coming from to make a work incentive plan a reality. Kennedy's own fully developed program was, of course, based on the premise that creating new jobs was the first priority in dealing with poverty anywhere. Nixon, who talked somewhat loosely about "black capitalism" both during his campaign and afterwards, would have felt the pressure to specify. And Kennedy might have been led to reconsider his aversion to the guaranteed income. There might, in short, have been a fruitful discussion of important ideas. And, again, the voters would have known the meaning of their votes.

Another instance of Richard Nixon's efforts at presidential leadership is his plea to purify and preserve the environment. In a message to Congress on February 10, 1970, the President offered a program containing thirty-seven points, of which twenty-three were new legislative proposals and fourteen were actions to be taken either by executive order or by existing administrative authority. It was an impressive package. The message covered all aspects of water and air pollution and dealt extensively with problems of conservation.

President Nixon's most severe criticism fell on municipalities for inadequate handling of sewage treatment and waste disposal, and his one substantial request to Congress for new money was for the building, expansion, or improvement of municipally owned disposal plants. The President's criticism of industry, especially the automotive, was less forceful, and his proposals amounted to little more than calling for more rigorous enforcement and nationalizing of existing minimum standards.[10] Congressional Democrats and others pointed out that Nixon's proposed expenditures were in fact less than what had already been appropriated for the purpose. But there was no denying that the President had brought together the many facets of the environmental problem effectively and that he had taken leadership on a vital and widely popular issue. His efforts, in fact, gave the strongest impetus the nation had yet had to reverse the frightening course of environmental debauchery.

What was regrettable, again, was that there had been little significant debate on the problems of ecology in the

1968 campaign. No doubt the candidates were not anxious to treat in detail an issue where there was no dispute as to purposes, yet where the measures needed not only involve often complicated questions of technological application but inevitably irritate important vested interests. From the point of view of sheer vote getting (or losing) Robert Kennedy's Oregon campaign was an object lesson. Not only were his appeals for reconciliation of the races and his radical attack on urban poverty poorly received among Oregon's largely affluent and nearly all white population, but so also was his direct attack on the environmental problem. In a speech at Portland, for example, Kennedy reminded his audience that pollution was rapidly advancing:

Already, the oxygen content is too low for fish to run up the Willamette. In the lower part of the river, where you once swam and fished, there is no life, and it is necessary to go above Oregon City to find clear water.

He proposed to deal directly with the problem:

The fact is that we can build Oregon's economy and attract industry, and at the same time control pollution and preserve the lakes and rivers for recreation. We have the technology to do this, and the only question is whether we have the will to plan now. It requires the effort of the local community, private industry and all levels of government . . . .

Had he stopped there no one could have taken exception, and the divisive core of the problem would have been left undisturbed. Instead he went on:

But the real initiative must come from your own effort—to modernize plant facilities so that waste disposal is controlled as effectively as possible; so that emission is cooled before being returned to the water; so that, as much as possible, industrial wastes are treated and reused instead of being dumped into rivers and streams.

More attention must also be given to the placement of industry along our rivers. . . . It is essential that we plan for future recreational needs—for once land is taken for another purpose, once the beauty of the countryside is spoiled, it cannot easily be restored.[11]

The results of the Oregon primary did not encourage this kind of talk.

Because everyone has a vital concern that the human environment be purified and preserved, there is the insidious danger that presidential efforts to educate and lead the people in this field may have the effect of obscuring other pressing and more divisive issues. For a time in 1970 even the antiwar protesters, reassured for the moment by the return of troops through "Vietnamization," seemed prepared to divert their energies to the ecological struggle. The invasion of Cambodia, however, jolted them back into antiwar activities.

From the perspective of the politics of presidential leadership there is some analogy between Nixon's approach to the environmental issue and President Eisenhower's leadership on the national highways program. Both programs were national rather than regional in their appeal. Both were to at least some degree to everyone's advantage. Both transcended class or racial differences. The parallel disappears only when the intrinsic importance of the ecological problem is considered. While people in the 1950s thought that a national highway system would be a desirable improvement in transportation and communication, as well as a politically expedient means of financing roads which local governments could not afford to build, there was no sense of crisis. Not so with the environment. Once the warnings of the ecologists were heeded it became, in the mordant words of the slogan, "a matter of life and breath." President Nixon thus found in the issue of pollution control a nearly unique combination of widely shared, nonpartisan urgency to act, with welcome political advantages.

The danger lay in preferring exploitation of the political advantages over response to urgent need. Building more and better waste treatment plants, important as it is, does not eliminate those causes of waste which could in fact be eliminated. Investing in prototype nonpollutant automobiles, pointing hopefully to the future, does not diminish the fumes of the present. Popular as the environmental issue is, in short, to manage it effectively the President must at some point make unpopular decisions. Industry has repeatedly shown its willingness, as the President said in his message, to invest in antipollution research and to experiment with antipollutants, but it has shown little disposition to adopt radically new and costly engineering or relocation plans in order to reduce or eliminate its waste products and air pollutants quickly. President Nixon's order, early in 1971, to enforce an old law penalizing those who dump wastes into lakes and rivers would depend for its efficiency on standards he carefully avoided spelling out. Such black leaders as the Reverend Ralph Abernathy may exaggerate when they suggest that the President placed heavy emphasis on the environmental problem in order to avoid radical action on poverty and discrimination;[12] but the imperative need is nevertheless for the President now and in the future, whoever he may be, to give leadership in the reconstruction of the whole of American society, as Kennedy proposed to do in 1968. Just as the grand design of a national highway system, popular and useful as it was, could not compensate for President Eisenhower's unwillingness to take leadership in the struggle against racial discrimination, with incalculably disastrous consequences for his successors, so President Nixon's broad and properly popular appeal to "clean up the environment" could not compensate for failures of leadership in rooting out the causes of social injustice and cultural and economic deprivation.

The style of a President is commonly if not always implicit in his campaign for the office. The frequently stodgy and sometimes trivial pronouncements of Franklin Roosevelt in 1932 were soon forgotten in the excitement of his dynamism in March of 1933. That dynamism had in fact been foreshadowed here and there in the campaign, notably in the Commonwealth Club speech.[13] But such brain trusters as Rex Tugwell were often driven to near distraction by Roosevelt's last minute substitution of stale platitudes for the fresh ideas in their speech drafts when political advisers warned him that the audience would not respond favorably to unusual proposals.[14] In retrospect it is easy to forget that Roosevelt was a consummate politician who always sought to start where the people really were and then move them forward, not strike out far in front of them and hope they would catch up. His opponents always thought him devious. As President, especially in his first term, he often relied heavily on improvisation, and sometimes on sheer rhetoric, to cover his uncertainty in economic matters. But as he gained confidence he was less nervous about accepting theoretically consistent, even radical ideas. The difference between his first and second campaigns was thus immense. And the vigorous, joyous partisanship and advocacy that characterized his speeches in 1936 set the style for his Presidency from his first reelection to the war years.

But it is not easy to break out of a pattern set in a successful campaign. President Eisenhower, for example, apparently did not wish to do so, at least until the last years of his second term when he found it almost impossible. In 1952 he relied on his immense popular reputation and campaign mixture of sharp, often pettish denunciation of inflation, corruption, and "bungling" with suggestions that such evils would be overcome simply by his election. The drift that characterized his administration derived in large measure from his popularity as a man "above politics" appealing to most of the diverse groups of American society. Marquis Childs once aptly called him a "captive hero"; he was captive of his own popularity.[15] Any serious attack on the accumulating problems of the nation would have offended important constituents and diminished his popularity. Liberal critics who took him to task for not expending some of his great store of "political capital" to promote progressive measures were off the mark. That capital was not spendable.

President Truman's problem was at the opposite extreme from Eisenhower's. As the vigorous partisan of specific programs, the capital he accumulated in personal popularity was identified with his partisanship. It was available for investment in the programs for which he campaigned. The trouble was that there was not enough of it. Neither Truman nor his program was popular enough. Eisenhower's popularity, on the other hand, was wholly personal and had little if anything to do with programs he proposed. At a moment of great national tension and concern he projected an image of quiet, genial, patient self-discipline. He could be trusted. The effect was almost analgesic.

At a moment of much greater national tension and concern Richard Nixon evidently sought to emulate the General, whom he had served as Vice President for eight years and unreservedly admired. Not only were there visible attachments to Eisenhower—the joining of the families by marriage, the visits to the General's sickbed—but the skillful effort to suggest the Eisenhower commitment to calm, dispassionate, stable government in Washington, to end a hated war, restore order to the turbulent streets, and stop the insidious inflation.

It was essential to a campaign grounded on an appeal to personal trust that the more divisive issues be touched with soothing or reassuring rhetoric, not to build support for a program but to secure confidence in the candidate's experience. His long service in the government, especially as Vice President in the nostalgic Eisenhower years, could be well enough matched by Hubert Humphrey with his many years of liberal leadership. But the appeal of a man rising from defeat, chastened and wise, could not. If he had once been brash and overconfident, Nixon had learned by suffering and was now fit, in the tradition of the General, to preside over the nation.

He opened his campaign, on February 3, 1968 in Concord, New Hampshire, with the promise of a new leadership to give the country "the lift of a driving dream" that would overcome a "crisis of the spirit."[16] (On the same day, perhaps fortuitously, Julie Nixon and David Eisenhower announced that they would be married even before they graduated from college.) In all the months thereafter, Nixon seldom spoke of what ought to be done, but often of the need to do it. In an address on the Presidency, toward the end of September, he spoke effectively of the nature of leadership:

There are occasions on which a President must take unpopular measures. But his responsibility does not stop there. The President has a duty to decide, but the people have a right to know why. The President has a responsibility to tell them—to lay out all the facts, and to explain not only why he chose as he did but also what it means for the future. Only through an open, candid dialogue with the people can a President maintain his trust and his leadership.[17]

The words were unexceptionable; indeed, they were directly appropriate to the needs of the nation. But the campaign gave no clear indication of what such unpopular decisions might be, no instances of what to expect of him as a "crisis-manager." Thus the dialogue Nixon commended could come only after the fact of a decision. His own experience, as President, with the consequences of his decision to go into Cambodia amply illustrates the entrapment of a President in the style of his campaign. That decision also, and perhaps more significantly, reveals the entrapment of the people when candidates are simply trusted to exercise wise leadership without having made clear what the nature of that wisdom might be. The disillusionment of many Americans with the Cambodia decision, after the months of growing trust of "Vietnamization" as evidence of intent to end the war, did more damage to the Presidency both at home and abroad than could possibly be overbalanced by military success in the venture.

The American presidential system is surely on trial, to see whether it cannot only survive but manage the crisis, domestic and international, the United States is facing. It was precisely the prospect of actions like President Nixon's Cambodia decision that led Robert Kennedy to run for President in 1968. As a Democrat and a believer in party loyalty he opposed President Johnson, first on issues and finally for office, only with the greatest reluctance. But his sensitivity to the thoughts and feelings of disenchanted young people, of the poor, and of the alienated minorities persuaded him that the system was failing. As he saw it, not only was President Johnson suffering from a loss of credibility but so also was the whole American commitment to democratic presidential government. This was why he said at the beginning of his campaign and often afterward, "I do not run for the Presidency to oppose any man, but to propose new policies.''

The ideas and programs Kennedy advocated were often divisive, and involved him in an uncomfortable paradox, as well as exposing him to political attacks on his capacity to govern. How can one divide the country yet reconcile hostile factions, classes, and communities? Simply to divide a nation is not a program. To divide it by stirring up animosities is contemptible. To mistake for reconciliation a temporary calm induced by soothing rhetoric or by a potential storm invites disastrous consequences. But to propose programs for striking at the causes of existing divisions is not incompatible with reconciliation—to the contrary, it is necessary if durable reconciliation is ever to begin. Herein lay the whole meaning of Kennedy's campaign, not only in its own time but for the present and the future.

What Robert Kennedy was saying in 1968, and what we have learned in the aftermath, is that presidential leadership —not presidential politics—is no longer merely desirable, it is imperative.

It will not do to hide neglect, however "benign," of one critical problem under a blanket of rhetoric about another. And dramatic presidential journeys across the world, even to China, will not reconstruct a decaying society.

It will not do to tell the people one thing about war or peace and mean another.

It will not do to crack down on crime and violence without addressing their causes.

It will not do to rally "hard hats" against protesting students.

Nor will it do to rally protesting students against the Establishment.

It will not do to blame one party for foreign war or domestic turmoil.

It will not do to say that the end of the war will not release the money needed to reconstruct the nation.

It will not do for the President simply to ignore the will of the Congress.

Nor will it do to dismantle the power of the President.

In their old age Thomas Jefferson told John Adams that he liked "the dreams of the future better than the history of the past."[18] If those dreams are not to be fearful, the American President—and the American Congress and the American people—will need to deal radically, and together so far as may be, with the present.

Notes

INTRODUCTION

1. Jack Newfield, *Robert Kennedy: A Memoir* (New York: E.P. Dutton, 1969), p. 304. See also Charles Reich, *The Greening of America* (New York: Random House, 1970).
2. President Nixon boasted, in his State of the Union message (1970), that the only agencies for which he was asking more money were those involved in fighting crime.
3. James Reston, *New York Times*, 2 January 1970, p. 36.
4. *The New Yorker*, 15 March 1969, p. 29.
5. Arthur Schlesinger, Jr., Address to Democratic Dinner, Chicago, 29 September 1968. Speech text.
6. I have examined the relation between Eisenhower's broad popularity and several major issues of his time in *The American Presidency: Leadership, Partisanship, and Popularity* (New York: Macmillan Co., 1966), pp. 99–111, 170–181, 239–248.
7. John F. Kennedy, Address to National Press Club, 14 January 1960. *New York Times*, 15 January 1960, p. 14.
8. Speech in New York City. *New York Times*, 7 October 1964, p. 37.
9. Speech in Rochester, New York. *New York Times*, 30 September 1964, p. 32.

VIETNAM AND THE DIRECTIONS OF FOREIGN POLICY

1. Douglas Ross, ed., *Robert F. Kennedy: Apostle of Change* (New York: Trident Press, 1968), p. 501.
2. See Sir Robert Thompson, *Defeating Communist Insurgency* (New York: Praeger, 1966) and *No Exit from Vietnam* (New York: David McKay, 1969).
3. See Arthur Schlesinger, Jr., *A Thousand Days* (Boston: Houghton Mifflin, 1965), pp. 497 ff., and Theodore Sorenson, *Kennedy* (New York: Harper and Row, 1965), pp. 731–745. Robert Hurley's doctoral dissertation, *President*

John F. Kennedy and Vietnam, University of Hawaii, 1970, marshals all the evidence and suggests the great likelihood that Kennedy was, at the time of his death, wholly disenchanted with the Vietnam adventure.

4. *Apostle*, p. 502.
5. Ibid., p. 503.
6. Ibid., p. 508.
7. Ibid., p. 510.
8. Robert F. Kennedy, *To Seek a Newer World* (New York: Bantam Books, 1968 [originally published by Doubleday, 1967]), pp. 162–163.
9. *To Seek*, p. 166.
10. Ibid., p. 168.
11. Ibid., p. 171.
12. Ibid., p. 177.
13. Ibid., pp. 189–190.
14. Ibid., p. 190.
15. Ibid., p. 190. For an informed and thoughtful review of American mistakes in Vietnam policy see Henry Brandon, *The Anatomy of Error* (Boston: Gambit, 1969).
16. Address at Kansas State University, 18 March 1968. Speech text, p. 5.
17. Ibid., p. 6.
18. *To Seek*, p. 110.
19. Ibid., p. 111.
20. Ibid., pp. 111–112. Kennedy would have been amused by the "ping pong" diplomacy of 1971, which seemed to open up opportunities for expanding American-Chinese relations, but he might have taken satisfaction in the Nixon administration's important change of policy.
21. Ibid., p. 112.
22. Ibid., p. 113.
23. Ibid., p. 117.
24. Address at the University of Indiana, 24 April 1968. Speech text, pp. 2–3.
25. See *The Rockefeller Report on the Americas* (Chicago: Quadrangle Books, 1969), pp. 21–35, 37–39, 55–65, 70–80.
26. *To Seek*, p. 160.
27. Address to Neveh Shalom Congregation, Portland, Oregon, 26 May 1968. Speech text, p. 1.
28. William Vanden Heuvel and Milton Gwirtzman, *On His Own: RFK 1964–1968* (New York: Doubleday, 1970), p. 389. The italicized lines were added in Kennedy's hand to his prepared reading text.

THE CITIES: POVERTY, RACE, AND CRIME

1. Douglas Ross, ed., *Robert F. Kennedy: Apostle of Change* (New York: Trident Press, 1968), p. 78.
2. Ibid., pp. 79–80.
3. Ibid., p. 78.
4. Ibid., p. 79.
5. Ibid., pp. 81–82.
6. Ibid., p. 93.
7. Ibid., p. 94.
8. Ibid., p. 95.
9. Ibid., p. 97.
10. Ibid.
11. Ibid., p. 237.
12. Ibid., p. 239.
13. All of the quotations in this section are taken from Robert F. Kennedy, *To Seek a Newer World* (New York: Bantam Books, 1968), pp. 20–43.
14. Speech of 10 April 1968. Kennedy text, p. 1.
15. Speech of 25 April 1968. Kennedy text, p. 3.
16. Address at street rally, Indianapolis, 4 April 1968. Kennedy staff transcript of extemporaneous remarks.
17. Speech of 10 April 1968. Kennedy text, p. 1.
18. Address at Gary, Indiana, 15 April 1968. Kennedy text, p. 1.
19. Ibid.
20. Ibid., p. 2.
21. Ibid., p. 3.
22. Address at Biltmore Hotel, Los Angeles, 19 April 1968. Kennedy text, p. 2.
23. Ibid., p. 3.
24. Address at Detroit, Michigan, 15 May 1968. Kennedy text, p. 1.
25. Ibid., p. 2.
26. Press release covering "A Program for the Urban Crisis," 31 May 1968. See also "A Program . . . ," p. 2. On 26 May Kennedy had issued a detailed program and recommendations for the involvement of business in poverty areas.
27. "A Program for the Urban Crisis," p. 9.
28. Ibid., p. 2. Also quoted for emphasis in covering press release.
29. *New York Times*, 2 June 1968, p. 64.

YOUTH, POLITICS, AND THE PRESIDENCY

1. Robert F. Kennedy, *To Seek a Newer World* (New York: Bantam Books, 1968), pp. 2–3.
2. Quotations in this section are from *To Seek*, pp. 4–15.

3. Speech at University of Alabama, 21 March 1968. Kennedy text, p. 2.
4. Speech at San Fernando Valley State College, 25 March 1968. Kennedy text, p. 2.
5. Speech at Denver City Auditorium, 28 March 1968. Kennedy text, p. 1.
6. Address at Oregon State University, Corvallis, Oregon, 18 April 1968. Kennedy text, p. 1.
7. Ibid., p. 2.

PRESIDENTIAL POLITICS

1. I have discussed the Court fight in relation to presidential leadership at length in *The American Presidency* (New York: Macmillan Co., 1966), pp. 111–120.
2. As reported in the *New York Times,* 12 April 1970, p. 1.
3. *The New Yorker,* 18 April 1970, p. 138.
4. See *The American Presidency,* pp. 101–111.
5. See *The New Yorker,* 8, 15, 22 November 1969. The articles were later gathered into a book, *Justice: The Crisis of Law, Order, and Freedom* (New York: Dutton, 1970).
6. All quotations from President Nixon's statement are taken from the text issued by the White House and reprinted in *U.S. News & World Report,* 6 April 1970, pp. 80–87.
7. Address at Binghamton, New York, 9 September 1964. Douglas Ross, ed., *Robert F. Kennedy: Apostle of Change* (New York, Trident Press, 1968), p. 61.
8. Robert F. Kennedy, *To Seek a Newer World* (New York: Bantam Books, 1968), p. 36.
9. For a useful analysis of the Indiana vote see William Vanden Heuvel and Milton Gwirtzman, *On His Own: RFK 1964–1968* (New York: Doubleday, 1970), pp. 348–349.
10. See Warren Moscow, *Roosevelt and Willkie* (Englewood Cliffs: Prentice-Hall, 1968), pp. 8–9.
11. The Tonkin Resolution is on p. 18471 of *The Congressional Record* for August 1964.
12. *New York Times,* 14 January 1965, p. 12.
13. Ibid., 8 April 1965, p. 16.
14. Ibid., 5 May 1965, p. 18.
15. McNamara Press Conference. *New York Times,* 17 June 1965, p. 1.
16. President Johnson's press conference. *New York Times,* 29 July 1965, p. 1.

17. Address to the Nation, 31 March 1968. *New York Times.* 1 April 1968, p. 20.
18. Speeches in New Hampshire as reported in the *New York Times,* 11 March 1968, p. 1.
19. *New York Times,* 2 August 1968, p. 1.
20. *New York Times,* 4 November 1969, p. 16. All quotations from this address are from the same source.
21. White House text. *New York Times,* 21 April 1970, p. 1.
22. Ibid.
23. All quotations from the Cambodia speech of 29 April 1970 are from the White House text as distributed by the Associated Press.

THE POLITICS OF PRESIDENTIAL LEADERSHIP: PARTIES, CANDIDATES, AND THE PRESIDENT

1. Adlai E. Stevenson, *Major Campaign Speeches, 1952* (New York: Random House, 1953), p. 9.
2. Ibid., p. 5.
3. For a detailed analysis of the 1936 campaign in relation to partisanship and presidential popularity see my *The American Presidency* (New York: Macmillan Co., 1966), pp. 160–170.
4. Speech to Press Gang Luncheon, San Francisco, 21 May 1968. Kennedy text, p. 1.
5. Message of 11 August 1969. White House text. *New York Times,* 12 August 1969, p. 1.
6. *New York Times,* 18 May 1968, p. 19.
7. Ibid., 1 August 1968, p. 18.
8. Ibid., 27 September 1968, p. 30.
9. Ibid., 26 October 1968, p. 1.
10. The White House text of the message was carried by the *New York Times,* 11 February 1970.
11. Address at Portland, Oregon, 23 May 1968. Kennedy text, pp. 1–2.
12. CBS "Face the Nation," 25 March 1970.
13. 23 September 1932. Text contained in Basil Rauch, ed., *Franklin D. Roosevelt* (New York: Rhinehart and Co., 1957), pp. 74–85.
14. Arthur Schlesinger, Jr., *The Crisis of the Old Order* (Boston: Houghton Mifflin, 1957), pp. 415 ff.
15. Marquis Childs, *Eisenhower: Captive Hero* (New York: Harcourt, Brace & Co., 1958).

16. Speech at Concord, New Hampshire. *New York Times,* 4 February 1968, p. 1.
17. Nationwide Radio Address, 19 September 1968. *New York Times,* 20 September 1968, p. 33.
18. Jefferson to Adams, 1 August 1816. *The Life and Selected Writings of Thomas Jefferson,* Adrienne Koch and William Peden, eds. (New York: Modern Library, 1944), p. 677.

Index

151